Thinking with our Ears

Limited Edition — Outside of Standard Print Run
This copy is part of a special edition, issued separately from the standard print run.

Enceladus Press
www.enceladus-press.com
contact@enceladus-press.com

Enceladus Press is distributed by
The MIT Press, Cambridge, Massachusetts

This work was originally published in French
under the title *Penser avec les oreilles*

Graphic design and layout: Wilfried Laforge

ISBN: 979-10-977824-2-9

Printed and bond by Présence Graphique,
Monts, France.

Enceladus Press is distributed by
The MIT Press, Cambridge, Massachusetts

Thinking with our Ears

François Noudelmann

Translated by Brian J. Reilly

TABLE OF CONTENTS

REMERCIEMENTS

I thank Sarah Kay, my interlocutor for these thoughts on sound, who allowed me to develop them in a seminar at New York University and through a conference we organized in 2017, *The Sense of Sound*. My thanks again to Georges Barrère, my first reader.

OVERTURE

Thinking is noisy. Ideas, signs, images ... none of these come to us on their own, but are mingled with sounds, if only we listen for them. The sonic dimension of thinking often goes unrecognized, for when we learn to read abstract texts, we tend to shut our ears. The recording and dissemination of seminars by certain thinkers has nevertheless recently provoked an interest in orality. Hearing the voice of Gilles Deleuze at the University of Vincennes, or Hannah Arendt's voice in a radio archive, or listening to a video-taped interview with Stanley Cavell provides new access to their thought, even if writing continues to be considered their thinking's most legitimate repository. More generally, studies devoted to the acoustic affordances of contemporary culture lead us to listen more carefully to these sonic realities, to the point of constituting a "sound turn" to counterbalance the domination of the visual. The emergence of *Sound Studies* in the United States and in Canada has now overflowed the disciplinary boundaries of cultural studies to reach anthropology, history, literature, and ecology. And yet philosophy still resists such an approach, having inherited a long tradition that considers sound a mortal danger to meaning. Against this willful deafness, I have undertaken this book to propose a new listening to texts in order to access unheard meanings.

The most obvious way we listen to thought, whether oral or textual, is through the voice. To hear and recognize a unique timbre encourages a personalization of thought: Simone de Beauvoir's voice or Vladimir Jankélévitch's can be identified from among the rest. When talking about a writer or philosopher's style or manner, we use the metaphor of their "voice." *That's her!, That's him!, That's them!*, we might say, recognizing their particular way of putting sentences together or advancing arguments. More theoretically, reflections on the voice often participate in the metaphysics of inspiration, where the voice would express a soul or manifest human exceptionalism. The voice captures our attention, erasing all other sources of noise nearby and thus testifying to the vococentrism of listening, whether in literature, film, or ordinary acoustic situations. This privileging of the voice, unfortunately, rests on many misunderstandings: First and foremost, believing that the absolute singularity of this or that speaker comes from the reduction of their voice to its timbre. And yet a good many other elements compose a voice, including, notably, elements that come from cultural, collective norms. Our accent, tone, and cadence are products of education, habit, and, above all, codes that lead us to speak at certain volumes and with certain vocalizations and rhythms depending on the circumstances. The "*author*" is not the owner of their voice, and, what's more, if we admit the psychic and social polyphony of *every* speaking being, *the* "author" has many voices. Despite our desire for unity, which would reduce the other's vocal spectrum to a single chord, good listening can allow us to perceive these different *me*'s in a single voice.

Even further, rather than pedantically interpreting *voices* of thought, we might find greater value in lending an ear more concretely to the sonic phenomena those voices emit. Then, rather than just majestic airs, we might hear noises that are slight or incoherent come to the fore, like breaths, cries, murmurs, and grunts. The speaker clears their throat, or there's a stutter, and suddenly the regular cadence of meaning gives way to unexpected syncopations revelatory of other meanings. Recording software often conceals these imperfections by eliminating the coughs and pauses of those speaking, even though that's where affects and latent thoughts slip through. Just as in writing where some sentences seem booming, others breathless, we might hear hesitation or haste behind the otherwise full and smooth speech of communicative language, leading to an entirely new listening.

Audio archives give us access to such symptoms, which must also be analyzed in terms of the acoustic devices that made them. Far from merely being a part of the history of technological progress, the machines that allow us to record, distribute, play back, and manipulate sounds, in particular voices, have profoundly modified our ways of speaking and listening, and thus of thinking. Using a phone, radio, or tape player is not just part of ordinary life. Through them, new perceptions, new ways of speaking, and new reflections have been developed. The use of such devices and machines directly inspired, for example: the soliloquy of Jean Cocteau's *The Human Voice*; the belches in Antonin Artaud's *To Have Done With The Judgment of God*; the passages on sonic consciousness in Maurice Merleau-Ponty's *The Visible and the Invisible*; and the routing of the self in Samuel Beckett's *Krapp's Last Tape*. Acoustic experiences can engender philosophical reflections and styles of writing. This happened to Jean-Paul Sartre, who changed the direction of his thinking and writing upon discovering the acoustics of the theater, the microphone at the radio studio, the megaphone in the street, or the personal recording device he used in his own musical practice. Myriad examples provide evidence that acoustic technologies have had a decisive influence on how we listen to the world, on our relations to others and to ourselves, and on our oral and written expression.

Though the voice is an integral part of sound, it cannot command all of our attention if we wish to hear the full spectrum of thought spread out in listening or reading.

Sounds, whether human or not, natural or constructed, intentional or random, accompany our reflections, shaping and sometimes directing them. Writers and philosophers occasionally allude to this, noting being bothered by a barking dog, the crack of a whip, or a revving motor, which keeps them from concentrating. But noises can also have a virtuous effect on their meditation, as did the cymbalization of cicadas for Socrates or the gurgling brook for Jean-Jacques Rousseau. These sonic phenomena, though they may at first seem anecdotal, bring forth unexpected motifs and inspire arguments and figures in ways instructive to point out. More broadly, the irruption of noise forms part of a sonic milieu we are not always aware of. Such noises form clusters in which images, words, and intellectual dispositions are forged. Without being types of music, they nonetheless compose "soundscapes" in which thought and imagination develop. Affinities thus arise through subtle arrangements between sounds and other sensible bodies, through connections between rhythms and ambient acoustics, between ideas and sentences. If a treatise or novel was written while its author listened to this or that piece of music, one should take account of all the noises that participated in its textual formation. I therefore propose a new undertaking that consists in locating, describing, and commenting on the soundscapes of thought.

The scope of such listening goes beyond the study of oral forms to attend to the sonority of writing as well. A methodological obstacle then seems to arise: How can we hear what is not acoustically perceptible? Yet the reading of a poetic text nevertheless brings forth sounds, like those produced by its rhymes without their needing to be read aloud. As long as we pay attention to signifiers, any text can generate sonorities through numerous phenomena attached to words, referents, rhythms, and many other elements that merit our exploration. If we admit that the imagination affords us visual quasi-perceptions, then we must recognize that there also exist auditory quasi-perceptions, as when we hear a tune "in our head" or as in many other situations, like reading a musical score, conversing with an interior voice, letting sound associations flow .... What we wrongly call *sound-images* come from virtual sounds that strike us, though, admittedly, less than images do, since such sounds seem less readily objectifiable. As a result, finding a text's sonorities consists in identifying, in writing, the echoes of the sounds that run through it, as well, in reading, the resonances brought about by a more or less active listening. Thus we hear the noises of a carriage as described by Madame de Sévigné or Marcel Proust. Nevertheless, we do not know exactly what such noise was in the sonic milieu of either era, nor do we have these writers' ears to listen to it with their individual sense of hearing. As readers, we unfold a virtual audio composition corresponding to our own acoustic milieu, to what our ears are used to hearing, to what our soul likes to hear sung.

Describing the soundscapes of thought allows us to hear them and understand them anew, for sonic modalities are also moral and political. Sartre held that writing a novel implicated the novelist's metaphysics, and Jean-Luc Godard declared that traveling shots are moral affairs — just as vocal ornamentation, orchestration, or acoustic environments are all matters of ethical responsibility, social relations, and worldviews. The recent movement of "sonic ecology" testifies to this, showing that the manner of inhabiting the planet as a universe of sounds reveals hierarchies, inequalities, and oppression. The omnipresence of commercial music in public spaces, the sound pollution surrounding a home near the highway, or the quest for silent spaces are likewise situations arising from a politics of sound. Almost a century ago, Theodor Adorno analyzed how the reign of materialist capitalism had profoundly upset our ways of listening. More recently, the writer Pascal Quignard pointed out the fascism of loudspeakers, as well as forms of resistance to the collective alienation of all-encompassing sound. With our bodies invaded by sounds not reducible to auditory phenomena, such auscultations of the world put into relief the philosophical and political importance of an attentive listening.

These critical listenings encourage us to lend an ear to sound arrangements in texts too, just as we do to the voices that "carry" thought. Writing contains the trace of a vocal posture, which it constructs even in the texture of sentences: In their amplitudes, measures, or excesses, readers can discern the voice addressing them as that of a master-thinker or one that trembles. In the enunciation of ideas, a libido may make itself heard, thereby affirming its power; it may seek to subjugate our ears, or, on the contrary, it might employ *mezza voce* suggestions. Arguments use a wide variety of registers according to whether they impose a univocal discourse or allow many voices to circulate in polyphonic multiplicities, or whether they rumble with murmurs and echoes, allowing other sources of sound and surrounding noises to permeate. Listening to a text is not only to be sensitive to its profusion of sounds, but also to perceive its dominant affects, its modes of disseminating meaning, the morals and politics of its discourse, which signal the type of relationship it seeks with its reader-cum-listeners. There is indeed a politics of the pensive voice and the sonic milieus present in texts.

Reading with our ears — that is this book's sound spectra. To our reading of signs, to our understanding and imagination, we must add a listening to sounds. Auscultating a text consists in charting sonic milieus and interrogating modes of listening. As long as a reader pays attention to them, a multitude of sounds, with varying statuses, resounds in texts, even those least intended to be noisy. Such an attitude invites us to take out the plugs we've put in our ears, as Nietzsche had asked us to do in denouncing the willful deafness of philosophy since its inception[1]. Nietzsche wanted us to listen to the music of the world. What's more, he himself was receptive to the timbre of each thought, boasting of having the most acute sense of hearing, which enabled him to discern the best thinking and the worst. What kind of a voice do we hear when we read a text? The author's? Our own? Or a virtual voice that depends on what we imagine to be the text's vocality, according to its age and echoes? Further, what sensitivities do we mobilize to perceive sounds and sound spectra? Since the start of the twentieth century there has been a manifest interest in sounds: At the heart of artistic avant-guards, composers became passionate about the spectrum of sound, and writers offered acoustic experiences through their texts. Nevertheless, such emphasis on sound cannot be summarized as a historical event, and we observe that, at many moments in history, there have been reflections and practices oriented to the world of sounds, whether in ancient Greek architecture, the Renaissance imaginary, or many other examples from diverse civilizations. What is novel instead comes rather from a new way of listening and the search for methods to reach these phenomena, particularly in disciplines like literary studies, history, anthropology, and political science. In the 1970s, the composer and theorist R. Murray Schafer attempted to furnish tools

1. Friedrich Nietzsche, *The Gay Science* (trans. Walter Kaufmann; Vintage, 1974), 372: "Having 'wax in one's ears' was then almost a condition of philosophizing; a real philosopher no longer listened to life insofar as life is music; he *denied* the music of life — it is an ancient philosopher's superstition that all music is sirens' music."

for such analysis, tools still fiercely contested today. More generally, we can take on his methodological effort in order to analyze "textual milieus," like literary and philosophical discourses.

Through this acoustic agenda, I wish to encourage a new relation to texts, which, read with our ears, reveal meanings that go beyond the ones intentionally constructed by their authors. Philosophers and psychoanalysts have sometimes intuited this kind of listening that would allow as yet unheard meanings to arise in the heart of a willed, controlled discourse. A "third ear" would thereby allow them to access ideas in the making, to reach the contradictory forge in which are mixed the affects, imaginations, and concepts that the text has arranged and set in place. A variable, musical, or acousmatic listening — depending on the acuity chosen — undoes the captivating power of explicit meaning and allows sounds at first unlocatable to rumble. A text then regains the chaotic mobility, the disordered dynamism that came before its composition, with its dissonances, disharmonies, and amalgams. The multiplicity of voices at the heart of a single discursive authority, the brouhaha of available meanings, the sonic milieus of thought then become audible. Those who would control meaning have always been afraid of such escapes, seeking to master their discourse by relegating all sound to the realm of nature or anecdote: *This is but the chirping of birds, turning our attention away from the main point*, thus do the learned warn us about the music of words. They were rather right to be wary, for sound — intangible and fleeting — escaped their grasp. And above all, listening to these suspect noises makes readers discover spaces and rhythms that allow them to read and understand differently, to hear certain philosophers' lies, to hear their obsessions, ecstasies, covert strategies, relations to the world, multiple personalities, etc. — all of which form the substance of their books.

I. The Willful Deafness of Philosophers

When we speak of music, or sound, or noise, what are we referring to? Despite the abundance of authoritative pronouncements about what separates music from an unbearable racket, there is neither physical nor aesthetic evidence that would afford a universal definition for any of them. Rather than propose a general theory, it would be better to look at the scope of references evoked by these words. We would thereby avoid maintaining that Music is ... or By nature sound is ..., and so leave space for an analysis of such notions according to their use in a given specific age or place. The qualification musical is not identical across cultures, and sound is not perceived in the same way by ears formed in different historical milieus. There are, however, continuities of meaning, recurring examples and images, which allow us to follow what specific groups of people mean by music or sound. This is true for philosophers as well, who, since ancient Greece, have made reference to music and sound on the basis of birdsong.

Do birds sing?

Why have birds been taken as the prototypical example of sound in the history of European philosophy? This choice is surprising, for we rarely listen to them for their "song," and, in their chirping, they incarnate counterfeit singers, emitting sounds devoid of sense. It is, moreover, difficult to know whether birds "sang" in the same way in the fifth century BCE as they do today, and, whatever could be said about the evolution of bird gullets, ancient Athenians surely did not listen to birdsong in the same way as someone out for a walk in the twenty-first century. The birds who chirp across the pages of ancient texts are rather imaginary birds whose sounds remain approximate and get associated with contemporary sounds. Their symbolic function nevertheless gives insight into the relations speechmakers had to song, to breath, and to sound. When birds are referenced, they rarely escape the symbolism of sacrifice — a rooster for Asclepius — or divination. So it was for Socrates, who, at the moment of death, compared his speech to a swan song. Against those who hear only suffering in such sounds, he reminds us that "no bird sings when hungry, cold, or in some other kind of distress, not even the nightingale herself, or the swallow or the hoopoe."[1] The foreknowledge of happiness after death, freed from material existence, is the unique cause of this song's beauty — so thought Socrates as he was leaving the prison of his own body.

The sound of birds thus obtains its worth at the price of being inspired by a divinity or an idea, without which it falls back into meaningless buzzing, the succession of onomatopoeias, like those Aristophanes made resound in his play *The Birds*. In Cloud Cuckoo Land, winged bipeds, especially the hoopoe, twitter on and on about the stupid blah-blah of the Athenians. The sounds sent forth by the birds in the time and place of Aristophanes come down to us thanks to the onomatopoeias transcribed by the playwright: "ἐποποποῖ, ποποποποῖ ποποῖ, ἰὼ ἰὼ ἰτὼ ἰτὼ ἰτὼ ἰτὼ ἴτω [...] τιο τιο τιο τιο τιο τιο τιο τιο [...] τριοτό· τριοτό· τοτοβρίξ. [...] τορο τορο τορο τοροτίξ κικκαβαῦ κικκαβαῦ τορο τορο τορο τορο λιλιλίξ."[2] Nevertheless, these transcriptions only bear witness to the way in which these noises were heard in a specific language and culture. The rooster's crow can be transcribed *Gaggalagaggalagó* in Icelandic, but *Mac na hóighe slán* in Irish — onomatopoeias say less about sounds than about the ears that hear them.

1. Plato, *Phaedo* (trans. Alex Long; Cambridge University Press, 2010), 85a.
2. Aristophanes, *Birds* (ed. Nan Dunbar; Oxford University Press, 1995), 227–62.

Bird cries provide a tuning fork to evaluate human voices as inspired discourse or artless noise. Song, when it carries no meaning, is mere eructation; the same goes for words and the language they employ. Brute sound, in itself, is limited to being only a vehicle for meaning, an acoustic phenomenon coming from the perceptible world, waiting to be understood. Disdain for sound stems from such a division, which metaphysicians would repeat for centuries to come, continuing to use their bird metaphors to maintain it. No surprise, then, that concrete interest for sound and vocality came from materialist thinkers. How does noise propagate? What is a voice? What do ears perceive? These questions, at first obscured by those systematic abstracting metaphysicians, come to find physical and philosophical answers. In his *On the Nature of Things*, Lucretius, fed by epicurean materialism, refined the theoretical stakes of these questions in a remarkable fashion, distinguishing the emission of sound from its audition, its meaning from its physics. Why is swan song immediately heard as a melancholic plaint, while a big trumpet blast produces a rough and barbarous roar? Before responding to the question of whether a sound or a piece of music by its nature expresses emotions — a problem philosophers and musicologists continue to debate today — we should know exactly how sound affects its listeners' ears.

Voice is sound

Rather audaciously, Lucretius does not presume any design for human bodies, and so our ears are no longer "made for" hearing. It simply happens that sounds, composed of material atoms, enter the ear canal and make hearing vibrate. The auditory effects, whether of a dreadful din or insidious chant, depend then on the qualities of these atoms, whether they are rough or soft. Regardless of the naïveté we see in such a physics today, what is at stake philosophically is the nature of sound freed from any metaphysical judgment. A radical consequence of such an approach is that the voice loses its exceptional status and becomes one sounds among others, with its particular vocal atoms. It is no longer treated as an exclusively human privilege and must be analyzed as an ordinary physical body, shared by many animals. Mouths allow us to articulate such matter and to represent elements of language, like words and tones. Perceiving a voice and understanding it depend less on the intention of the speaker than on the possibility of its atoms to remain concentrated and pierce the hearing of the listener[3], at the risk of scattering and hitting other auditory canals.

Argumentatively, Lucretius insists on the physical laws of sound to denounce vocal illusions people thought to be divinely inspired, for all could be explained materially — the confusion or clarity, depth or projections of a voice — without recourse to belief. What Lucretius was referring to when making fun of such superstitions are acousmatic phenomena, which is to say sounds we perceive without discerning their source. Echoes thus follow from the refraction of sound atoms on solid bodies, like mountains or walls, and not from the nocturnal noises of pans, nymphs, or fauns.[4] The credulous country folk's enchantment with voices is shared by the learned metaphysicians who also populate nature with supernatural voices. It is difficult, Lucretius observed, to admit that the materialist

3. Lucretius here takes up a description devised by Epicurus in his *Letter to Herodotus*, 53, in *Diogenes Laertius, Lives of the Eminent Philosophers* (ed. James Miller and trans. Pamela Mensch; Oxford University Press, 2018), Book 10.
4. Lucretius, *On the Nature of Things* (trans. W. H. D. Rouse and rev. by Martin F. Smith; Harvard University Press, 1992), 4.580.

explanation of voices and more generally of sounds is the only one and to lose the illusions of music or harmony created by hidden higher beings.

In his concrete analysis of sound, Lucretius proposed a method that has not lost any of its relevance: describe first, rather than interpret. Rather than propounding on the human voice, it would be better to know what voices really are and how they are audible. Understanding only comes after. Such an approach implies forgetting any metaphysical or aesthetic hierarchies of sounds produced by human means and so-called natural sounds, either from non-human animals or those unintentional noises of the sound environment. We would listen to the wind in the branches, the crash of a falling tile, a particular meowing just as we would to the voice of a soprano or public orator. Their atoms infiltrate everything, going through the walls that visual simulacra cannot cross. Lucretius's descriptions make us smile; nevertheless, they largely grasp the scope and course of sound: Unlike sight, hearing objectifies what it hears with great difficulty, for the listening subject is immerged in a sound setting that invades it through the ears. Intrusion, immersion, passivity, dispersion — these are the phenomenal qualities of sound that imply an entirely different relation to the world than obtains for vision. This hardly controllable infiltration explains, no doubt, the reserve, indeed the fear, of thinkers whose projects consist of objectivizing the real and mastering it by giving it a language and a meaning.

Attention to sonic matter was systematically devalued by metaphysicians, who relegated sound to the categories of rubbish or ruse. Nevertheless, the impossibility of not hearing, even after having plugged their ears with wax, obligated them to deal with sound, to direct it so that it would make meaning resonate as faithfully as possible.

In many discussions, we can see a struggle with this risk of dissonance. Sound, as materialists had noted, is confused, disparate, spread out, tortuous ...; it requires constant effort in order to grasp it. Dirty, inept, unruly — thus does sound appear to most philosophers. In the well-known antitheses of metaphysics, sound is grouped logically with what is natural, perceptible, animalistic, illusory, superficial, and disordered. Despite this rejection, sound continues to annoy these thinkers, who cannot stop themselves from hearing it when they speak, listen to speech, or even while they read texts. There's a sound, and then the sound resounds, and that is distracting ... unreasonably distracting.

Socrates the flute

Through a few classical references from philosophy, we observe this ambivalent relation of metaphysicians to sound, to music, and to the voice. The foundational move of any metaphysics is differentiation: separate, classify, and put into a hierarchy. There is good music and bad music: on the one hand, there is the right voice, the correct accent, the perfect rhythm, a beautiful harmony; on the other, there is vulgarity and facile and inane pleasure. A scene from Plato's *Symposium* establishes these motifs of conflict through the character Alcibiades, who arrives drunk among the guests gathered around Socrates. Called upon to praise this philosophical master, he believes it is wise to compare him to the satyr Marsyas, who plays the *aulos*. Socrates the flutist — this might seem an unexpected suggestion, though it would certainly come to be justified given that, before dying, Socrates would indeed express regret at not having learned to play the flute. Nevertheless, Alcibiades proposes a much more perilous and sacrilegious comparison, asserting that Socrates did not even need the instrument, for he himself was a flute! His words exercised an irresistible charm, and, like musical melodies, they troubled his listeners and took them over: "For whenever I hear him, my heart leaps even more than the Corybantes and the tears flow as a result of his words."[5] On Plato's account, Alcibiades's stupidity is thereby uncovered, as he hears discourse not for its meaning but for its sounds. His stupidity is coupled with a danger that menaces listeners who lack concentration. For such listeners, whenever sounds betray the speaker's intention, their attention is diverted away by the music of the discourse. The example of birds usually comes up again to name this type of misunderstanding: Instead of listening to intelligible speech, an idiot hears only birdsong. And so the flute is appropriate here because, unlike the lyre, it is like a type of bird. In this sonic imaginary, the flute joins with all things that involve breath and wind. Blowing and hissing, instead of articulating, the flute is reminiscent of animal cries. His comparison of Socrates to a flute thus underscores Alcibiades's tin ear and his inability to hear literal meaning. He is not a philosopher, but a music lover, putting him among the frivolous who heed the wind.

How, then, can the voice be made an instrument that does *not* betray the meaning of its speech? Although it is activated by air, the voice must not at all behave like a flute. Musical instruments more generally remain suspected of corrupting the meaning of the speech they accompany. When used alone, they are limited to entertainment, but when they are linked to speech, they risk doing it a disservice. Plato gives the lyre or zither a little more credit than the flute, so long as they follow the score rigorously and

5. Plato, *The Symposium* (in *Lysis, Symposium, Phaedrus*, trans. Chris Emlyn-Jones and William Preddy; Harvard University Press, 2022), 215e.

thus, through serious, cultivated art music, teach us rules of measure and harmony. Chords win out against winds, Apollo over Marsyas. The volatile air that carries the voice by necessity must thus be domesticated, corseted, in order to transmit the breath of reason[6] and not mimic the melodies that flow from flutes.

Singing among men

Plato's remarks on the voice, song, and music are founded on a strict objective: to interrogate sound, contain it, and put it at the service of meaning. As a result, this metaphysician recommends an extreme distrust of musical pleasure, which flatters the ears with vibrations as powerful as they are meaningless. These sounds give the illusion of structure, but they are devoid of content, like sounds emitted by birds. They come from whistling lips, not true breath. The history of philosophy and of literature shows that whistling remains associated with nonsense. This discrediting of whistling, which drags the voice down to bird cries and to animality, can be seen to continue, for example, in Charles Baudelaire's mockery of Northern whistlers[7] or Theodor Adorno's despondency at people being allowed to whistle Beethoven symphonies in the subway. A good upbringing continues to recommend against whistling or inappropriate breathing. Whistlers and flutists are, in effect, seducers who could lose their listeners in nonsense, just as the Pied Piper led children to their deaths.

6. Plato, *Republic* (ed. and trans. Christopher Emlyn-Jones and William Preddy; Harvard University Press, 2013), 394d: "ὁ λόγος … πνεῦμα."

7. Charles Baudelaire, "Pauvre Belgique" (in *Juvenilia, œuvres posthumes, reliquiae*, ed. Jaques Crépet and Claude Pichois; Éditions Louis Conard, 1952), 3:31: "Belgians are a whistling people, like stupid birds. What they whistle is not a tune."

Consequently a pedagogical philosophy would work to counter this type of seduction, which, true to its etymology, otherwise diverts the message so that it is addressed instead only to the pleasure of the ears. Such a philosopher takes care to control their breath and regulate their voice, making material vocal chords accord with abstract intellection. In *Laws*, Plato appreciates that song could play a role at the heart of the good city, and so he does allow music to be present there, but with extreme vigilance toward the voice, which must never fall back into "animal cries."[8] The guiding principle of good musical practice is to always make distinctions and put sounds into hierarchies according to age, sex, and social rank. Legislation privileges male choirs, with middle-aged men assuring that the younger be guided, for these men would know how to reject anything related to women's music, slave music, or lascivious or rustic music. Rectitude governs collective singing, unlike the choirs of tragedy where the voice gets divided into plaints and threnodies. Plato's model is a unanimous hymn of praise where no individual creates any division. Singular and correct, full and firm, masculine and controlled — that's what a good vocal organ should be.

Despite the structural virtue of music that could teach rhythm and harmony to good souls, its power remains suspect. Reading the passages where Plato attempts to integrate music into his legislative order, we can observe his constant difficulty in compartmentalizing its dimensions, which indeed proves impossible. He recognizes, in fact, that music, among all the arts, is the most captivating. Consequently, he asks that music emphasize speech and favor the practice of the good. But then, why not be content with words alone, without recourse to mediation by rhythm

8. Plato, *Laws* (trans. R. G.Bury; Harvard University Press, 1926), 669e.

or melody? Moreover, though keeping to his ambition for purely rational access to meaning, Plato remains confronted by the sonority of speech itself, even when it is not "put into music," for it is impossible not to hear in speech some noise that exceeds its content. One would have to read speech instead, plugging one's ears and silencing the tongue, but this attempt too is doomed to fail for even the text's speech rattles despite such efforts. Worse still, to this perceptual dimension is added a still more complex one: emotion. Emotion incites our desire to dance, cry, or love. It can be beneficial if the "soul is emotionally affected"[9] when this supports moral actions and orients the youth toward the ideas of the True, the Good, and the Beautiful. Yet when emotions derive from listening to music, they depend more on the beauty of its sounds than that of its ideas. For Plato, it is then no longer about differentiating good music from bad, but, more profoundly, it is about controlling the emotions linked to listening to sounds — a hope doomed to fail.

Constructed through this program of sonic education was the mental apparatus that would, for a long time to come, lead metaphysicians and other philosophers to willful deafness. And, as it is difficult not to hear anything, their remarks on music and sound would continuously bear witness to an unease that reason couldn't contain. Plato discredited the perceptible as a path to the intelligible in vain. Enjoined to see the invisible behind the visible, he could not render discourse inaudible, and so he had to come to terms with noises and the emotions they provoke. The result is that the listener is engaged in a perpetual struggle when listening to speech. Instruments will always be subaltern, music constantly suspect. The well-educated listener will hear only harmonious rhythmic structures, but

9. *Ibid.*, 812c.

still will not enjoy them. This listener will concentrate only on the messages and models they serve and will direct any emotions toward achieving a suprasensible truth, which would make no further sound. Good listening, on this account, paradoxically requires sacrificing one's ears.

In the dualist division made by metaphysicians, sound comes from nature, for it is perceptible through the sense of hearing. Just as they had for painting, they tried to relegate music strictly to the domain of the perceptible and of imitation. Unfortunately, it is difficult to reduce music to a mimetic art, unless it is thought to imitate animal cries. It is, moreover, on this point that philosophical theories of the arts fail, for any analogy between the visual and the audible does not hold. A painting of a bird does indeed present a reproduction of the bird, but a melody played on a flute does not immediately reflect birdsong, still less if played on a lyre. The Platonic theory of simulacrum cannot be applied to sounds. Consequently, if one must, at all costs, find a model for the arts, and if music cannot find its model in nature, its origin is an ungraspable artifice. Where does it come from? What is it really saying? Nothing tangible. Disappointment like this flows through Hegel's writings on music, which double down on Platonic ambivalences. Hegel nevertheless grants each art a place in his lectures on aesthetics, distinguishing among them by the manner in which they deploy the Soul's strength and transfigure reality. He defines their subjects, forms, and content, emphasizing those arts that express the spiritual with the most substantial content. And yet, music will resist so systematic a categorization.

The temptation of beautiful song

In the chapters he devotes to music, Hegel seeks its lost content. Unable to assume a specific materiality for sound or recognize some inherent meaning to sonic forms, he cannot grasp what music is. Substance and content, he believes, can only be added to it. In comparison to the other arts, like architecture, sculpture, or painting, Hegel asks: What does music embody? How does music externalize an idea? Intractable, music slips between his fingers, slides through the web of his thought. This failure to objectivize music — as though there were no sound "objects" — leads him to theorize it in terms of interiority.[10] He hears only tremors (*schwingenden Zittern*), only vibrations veering to one side or the other, without consistency or guiding principles. Music, materiality without material, thus cannot represent anything. Lacking objective exteriority, music presents only pure subjectivity. For all that, music, according to Hegel, is not so removed from Spirit, placing it in the same category as infinite interiority.

Expressive and interior, music, on Hegel's account, comes from something other than itself; it serves our feelings — terror, grief, joy, etc. — and gives them artistic resonance. Thus "the simple cry is analysed into a series of notes, into a movement, the change and course of which is supported by harmony and rounded into a whole by melody."[11] Musical forms enable us to put anarchic, elusive sounds into a straitjacket and control them with our minds. Musical forms thereby transform emotions and their meager content by giving them an autonomous interiority. Herein lies all of music's ambivalence: On the one hand,

10. G. W. F. Hegel, *Hegel's Aesthetics: Lectures on Fine Art* (trans. T. M. Knox; Oxford University Press, 1975), 892: "object-free inwardness."
11. *Ibid.*, 938.

music elevates; on the other, it escapes. The listener can surrender themselves to bliss, forgetting what the melodic air expresses and deluding themselves into finding a vague enjoyment in this sonic game despite this music's being "empty and trivial."[12] Hardly surprising, then, that, to illustrate sound devoid of sense, Hegel takes up the prototypical example: the bird! "The bird on the bough or the lark in the air sings cheerfully and touchingly just in order to sing, just as a natural production without any other aim and without any specific subject-matter, and it is the same with human song and melodious expression."[13] Or that he takes aim at Italian music and *art for art's sake*. Or, again, that he denounces sounds that tickle our ears and cease to have any relation to the meaning they are meant to express. Good music, instead, requires meaning, content (even if external), text, depth, as befits the "strict German musical intellect,"[14] thus Bach, Handel, the *lieder* ....

Such a repartition, so typical of metaphysical distinctions, nevertheless takes on an original tonality if we lend our ears to the tensions it covers over. Hegel in fact oscillates between devaluing and appreciating musical art that is instrumental and independent of any content. He admits the genius of composers who invent harmonies or rhythmic and melodic sequences appreciated by connoisseurs. Nevertheless he quickly expresses reservations and points out the risks of artistic subjectivity, its arbitrariness, caprices, and deceptions. This back-and-forth bears witness to the complex relation the person who listens, thinks, and writes has to the enjoyment they experience. Hegel compares music to the other arts and, for sake of contrast, extols poetry, which attaches sound to meaning. Music, on the contrary,

12. *Ibid.*, 940.
13. *Ibid.*
14. *Ibid.*, 949.

captivates the soul without furnishing it with meaningful content. It stirs our emotion by means of surging sounds that the listener is not free to control, subject instead to the magical power of the Sirens.

How could Hegel describe so precisely and so frequently this seduction by sonic forms if he did not, from time to time, respond to their call? To fully understand the contradictory forces that fuel a text like Hegel's, we must free ourselves of clichéd vocabulary and inquire into the practices and references underlying them. We should first ask: What kinds of music did Hegel listen to? Which kinds delighted him, even if they did not correspond to his intellectual ideals? The trip Hegel took to Vienna in 1824 tells us a bit. Despite the triumphant appearance of Beethoven's *Ninth Symphony* there and then, our philosopher doesn't say a word about it. The absence of references to Beethoven in his texts is, moreover, surprising given how much his readers are tempted to associate Hegel's thought with the powerful symphonies of this composer who seems the incarnation of Spirit. Still, what is most astonishing is his enthusiasm, confined to his correspondence, for *The Barber of Seville,* which was also performed at that time, and that he said he appreciated it even more than *The Marriage of Figaro*. Rossini over Mozart! Try deducing that from Hegel's seminars on aesthetics! Schumann attempted to give an explanation, proffering the theatricality, and so visuality, of opera, which would be more attractive to philosophers, given their greater immersion in the visual and verbal than in the audible. Even so, Hegel admits that he loves pure song, which he again compares to a bird on its branch. It sings just to sing, and nothing is more beautiful ... or rather "pleasant," for one must not let oneself be too much under its spell.

A guilty and tragic pleasure
Such an ambivalence regarding listening bears witness to the formidable temptation to which sounds subject philosophers' ears. The escape from meaning and the enjoyment of sounds for themselves present a fatal danger, which must be met with drastic reasoning and ethics. This type of sin pertaining to the meaning of words had already been described by Augustine in his *Confessions* when evoking his pleasure in listening to the songs of the mass:

> The pleasures of sound had captivated and enthralled me more powerfully, but you have released and liberated me. Nowadays, I admit, I find a degree of calm contentment in the sounds that your words bring to life when they are sung in a pleasing and skillful voice.[15]

Auditory pleasure, difficult to suppress, becomes the object of an admission, a confession, a regret. To justify this pernicious penchant for melodies and vocal timbres, Augustine recalls that they were also at the origin of his conversion to Christianity. The songs of the Church indeed brought tears to his eyes, showing that emotion was linked to reason. He quickly assures us that it was the *meaning* of the words that motivated his enthusiasm, as though he needed to rein in this passion for song to guarantee that song itself had not provided his true motive in moving toward God. Augustine expresses an ambivalence akin to that of the philosophers who are at once charmed and annoyed at having been carried away by sounds, seduced by them and diverted from the meaning of words. This passage from the *Confessions* is striking for its constant hesitation, its reversals from line to line, moving from concessions to retractions. "I am torn," he realizes, going back and forth.

15. Augustine, *Confessions* (trans. Carolyn J.-B. Hammond; Harvard University Press, 2014), 10.33.

His style is in permanent oscillation between searching for auditory pleasure and concentrating on the message alone contained in the Psalms. This would require using a neutral voice, without inflection, as well, surely, as forgetting their music, for, becoming aware of it, the listener would sin by their distracted hearing. This ideal of a tone that is specific, fitting, and appropriate to a meaning doubtlessly remains an illusion of will, perhaps a remnant of bad faith. At the end of his line of reasoning, Augustine maintains the need for singing, but he seeks a perverse pleasure in song that necessitates the listener's punishment after having enjoyed it.

The principal traits of willful deafness thus stem from a temptation. To the ears of metaphysicians — philosophers and theologians — music and, more fundamentally, sound seem like diabolical powers, which is to say separating powers. They divert meaning; they are freed from reason and unduly acquire their autonomy. They are Sirens attracting voyagers who listen to them, causing them to change course. The man of reason, like Odysseus, asks to be secured, bound to the mast to continue on his way, straight ahead, and orders the rowers to plug their ears with wax. Philosophy must resist sound in this way; it must hear nothing, focus on its aims, and ignore the sonorities of its prose. To reflect in silence, as if praying in one's innermost being, is to aim for a degree zero of sound to which the servants of the *logos* aspire, whether for the world of ideas or the kingdom of God.

Unfortunately one has to leave one's ears open in order to converse with others, even to advise blinkers or ear trumpets. When the weather turned hot, Socrates, chatting with his disciples in the open air, could not help but perceive cicadas cymbalizing or chirping around him, disturbing his dialogue. He thinks he knows the mischief they're up to, suggesting that they like to make fun of philosophers if they see them nonchalantly lying down to listen to their song. But, since Socrates could not give in to this temptation, he allows himself neither the idleness of slaves nor — yet another derogatory comparison — the gregariousness of sheep. He resists, he ignores them and remains deaf to their perturbing noises: "They see us talking and sailing past them as if immune to the Sirens' spell."[16] Nevertheless, he gives them enough importance to construct a legend and a lesson about them. According to an old story, at the moment the Muses appeared, and with them the art of song, humans took such pleasure in listening to them and in singing themselves that they lost their appetites, to the point that they died of thirst and hunger. They were then transformed into cicadas, a race that doesn't need food but can sing non-stop. Nevertheless, these insects would thereafter have the job of reporting back to the Muses conversations among humans so that the Muses could favor those who honored them, which is to say those who used the music of their speech wisely. From this legend we see that resistance to sound constitutes a test used to judge a person's worth: Unrepentant singers lose their humanity and become insects; on the other hand, those who know how to modulate their speech without singing but with proper emphases stay on the path of reason and merit praise. And as for the good among the faithful, they must, like Augustine, use sounds without enjoying them. To not listen to noise and to speak with the least amount of singing — these two injunctions establish the appropriate attitude to reason and to faith.

16. Plato, *Phaedrus* (in *Lysis, Symposium, Phaedrus*, trans. Chris Emlyn-Jones and William Preddy; Harvard University Press, 2022), 259a–b.

The fight against the separatory voice is without end, an eternally recurring ordeal against the temptation of sound. Neutralizing the voice, making it speak without making a sound, such is the impossible mission of master discourses against the natural tendency of any voice to break free of its words' contents. For the tragic fate of speech resides in its ineluctable vocality, which, even in the most neutral tone, renders discourse corporeal and perceivable. Some grain always remains, which gives ideas a unique tonality, resistant against voiceless universality. Voice is a continual transfer, and speech, even speech that is not sung, cannot be freed of the verbal sounds it pronounces when speaking, even internally. Tragedy begins in vocality, and it is fulfilled necessarily by the unwilling speaker. The learned, who are willfully deaf, condemn those who give in without fighting against becoming mindless beings, like birds or insects. Consequently, the discipline necessary for speakers and listeners is to adopt neutrality in tone without affect or, when it comes to music, to respect strict harmonic rules. The praise of harmony by many philosophers harmonizes with this discipline, for harmony offers a structure that allows the sonic and perceptible multiplicity to be contained. This appeal takes its place in a series of measures that aim to domesticate voices, whether by the murmuring of prayer, by interior and silent reading, or by the construction of musical chords. It would take a thinker-musician like Rousseau to harmonize heart and the power of truth and to privilege melody over harmony in the famous conflict between Italian music and French music. Rousseau distrusted deaf and mute reason and put his full faith in emotion carried by song. But he was an exception in this choice of the melodic, a choice rarely claimed by philosophers.

Sound seems unruly to the ears of metaphysicians. And, by metonymy, animalistic, mindless, divisive, seductive .... Their heroic efforts to arraign sound come up against their failure to understand it, whether music or noise. Jacques Derrida, who sought to deafen the great thinkers with noise, wondered, "can one puncture the tympanum of a philosopher and still make oneself heard by them?"[17] As prisoners of a monological conception of meaning, philosophers don't allow themselves to hear sound for itself, in its materiality and its meaning. Nevertheless, the interest of their remarks on sound comes from the tension they express between, on the one hand, turmoil, enjoyment, and emotion, and, on the other, inhibition, control, and authority. Auditory pleasure seems immoderate to them, since it pulls them so strongly toward excess. Whence this excitement over a piece of music? Why does it provoke tears? And, most of all, how is it that, even if you change the meaning of a song's words, the emotion can remain intact? This escape from meaning revolts minds who hold to language's univocity. And yet, they speak, rationalize, and try to protect themselves, all the while admitting, despite themselves, their weakness and incomprehension. They denigrate sound, rejecting it as volatile animality; they close themselves off to its power by plugging their ears; they incarcerate it in a hierarchical order by distinguishing music from sound; they disenchant it by crushing voice and instrumentation under the weight of words. Sound is their blind spot, or rather their blank note (*note sourde*). Perhaps the history of philosophy would have taken a totally different route had Socrates played the lyre, which, according to Diogenes Laertius, he attempted to do at the end of his life.

17. Jacques Derrida, *Margins of Philosophy* (trans. Alan Bass; University of Chicago Press, 1982), xii. Translation modified.

II. The Auditory Turn in Philosophy

Sound is an unruly material that philosophers have tried in vain to channel. Disarmed by this power that they cannot objectify, they come to envy architects who, aided by the science of acoustics, figured out early on how to construct spaces that allowed them to control sound and thus our listening. The theater of Epidaurus is often cited as a model, though one should add those ancient architectural designs for surveillance, like the grotto at Syracuse called the Ear of Dionysius, thanks to which tyrants could listen in on seditious talk. From early on, the skill of controlling sound served spy craft as much as art. As a power play, this mastery over sound aims to gather secret speech or to enter into people's ears in order to go to work on their bodies. Used as a weapon of war, soldiers' war cries were associated with trumpets sounding battle, with the aim of terrorizing the enemy's ears. Philosophers, less bellicose, but still mindful of molding their disciples' souls, conceived of the ears as receptacles for words of reason. They wanted to discipline the sounds that would enter ears and to fashion the canals that would receive these sounds. The way philosophers speak about hearing reveals their philosophy.

Born from the ear

The art of philosophical discussion, however, modified the approach to sound. It became distinct from teaching by lecture, where the listener is reduced to an acoustic funnel into which learned words are poured. Listening to the other speak is exactly what provokes attention to the tones, delivery, and rhythms of their voice and comes to highlight the opacity of meaning. Far from the illusory Socratic dialogue where the interlocutor is guided on the path toward truth, discussion allows unexpected ideas to come forth, which get modified in the back-and-forth among many mouth and many ears. In the Renaissance, Rabelais gave us a literary allegory that showcases this essential role of hearing in culture: the extraordinary birth of his character Gargantua from the ear of his mother. She had been suffering from diarrhea, and the medicine administered to her was so astringent that it blocked the natural exit. Gargantua, that soon-to-be giant of polymorphous desires, instead ascended his mother's body and, after traveling through several organs, found a better way out: the ear canal. This literary character comes into being through the ear and then manifests limitless curiosity for a world called *renascent* that was then opening itself up to so much knowledge. Yet such a delivery strains the symbolic load of listening, and the issuing of the child from inside the body to outside suggests a decisive reversal: While the ear is traditionally an organ of passivity, the place where the noise of the world slips in unbeknownst to the listener who is condemned to undergo a continual violation of their silent inner self, this time it is the ear that makes something come forth, competing with other orifices. Gargantua refused to be born in his mother's excrement, nor did he come out of her mouth like some new words of annunciation, nor was he regurgitated from her stomach. Thereafter, the ear was an active organ, and Creation could have been radically different had it pleased god to bring forth children in this way. The Rabelaisian parody of the Annunciation — Mary received the news of her conception from the voice of an angel coming in through her ears — suggests a new *conception* of listening, one that is active and directed toward the outside. Listening allows us to analyze, to receive that which gives meaning and transforms existence. Each person must be free to listen in their own way, especially to the divine word, for each ear is drawn singularly and actively toward the sounds of the world.

A few decades later, another Renaissance writer, Montaigne, accorded a major role to hearing, more important than that of sight. Unlike philosophers who associated thought with vision, Montaigne privileged hearing. As both French and English allow us to say, *entendre* 'to hear' means to perceive auditorily as well as to understand intellectually: *Je vois bien / J'entends ce que vous dites*, 'I see / I hear what you are saying'. While the history of philosophy has discussed at length the proximity, seen in Plato and in Ancient Greek, between *idea* and *eidos*, between forms, ideas, and the visible, it has hardly analyzed the link between the thinkable and the audible. And yet, since antiquity, the procedures of philosophy have largely entailed orality, whether in the form of dialogue or instruction. The sonic dimension of thought has been underestimated even though the means of exchange have decisive importance on the very content of philosophy. The tone of their voices, the distance between speakers, the posture of the listeners, the acoustics of the setting — the Stoa, for example, is not the Garden, and the Garden is not the Academy, etc. — all of these circumstances participate in the philosophical exercise. They establish a politics of conversation, according to which they organize the acoustic hierarchy of speakers and the circulation of sounds. Montaigne takes up this soundscape of thought, a medium for disputation and progress in understanding, and he affirms: "The most fruitful and natural exercise of our mind, in my opinion, is discussion."[1] Montaigne underscores that philosophy is more a way of living than the solitary writing of abstract treatises and that it engages an active relation with interlocutors, as Pierre Hadot and Michel Foucault in the twentieth century would need to

1. Montaigne, *Essays* (trans. Donald Frame; Stanford University Press, 1958), 3.8, 704.

remind us. Though he consulted books more than anyone else, Montaigne did not for all that prefer any less oratorical jousts that simultaneously instructed and inspired. And to clearly note the sonic stakes of conversation, he declared: "If I were right now forced to choose, I believe I would rather consent to lose my sight than my hearing or speech."[2] The prevalence of conversation contradicts the association of thought with silence. It suggests instead that thinking is a matter of listening, a matter of voices and noises.

Speaking, listening, hearing each other — these are the elements of philosophical conversation. The way one projects one's voice, whether exerting it at a particular moment of the argument or nuancing it to seduce, participates in the art of conversation just as much as any method of communication. The reflections of ancient thinkers on the eloquence of orators, philosophers, or politicians, as distinct from the eloquence of actors, helps us master such skills.[3] Montaigne, who was rather modern for this attention to the conditions of speech and to the effects of meaning induced by acoustics, was aware that he spoke too loudly. He was often asked to moderate his volume, and, via reference to the ancient philosopher Carneades who suffered from the same defect, he wondered what the best voice for him to use was. Good sense supposes an acoustic equilibrium between the voice that speaks and the ear that hears, such that the speaker should always adapt to the listener. Nevertheless, Montaigne preferred to accept his loud voice, which he used as a weapon to enter into the body of the other, to hit them and to pierce them. He even claimed to have many voices, as one has many strings on

2. *Ibid.*
3. See Florence Dupont, *L'Orateur sans visage* (Presses Universitaires de France, 2000).

a bow: the voice that instructs, the voice that flatters, the voice that scolds, and so on. The listener need only keep a distance to resist these acoustic jousts. Montaigne concludes: "Speech belongs half to the speaker, half to the listener."[4] The generosity of this reflection is stunning and contravenes arguments from authority. Meaning does not belong to the speaker's intention, but also depends on its reception. Which is to say that the meaning of words pronounced is suspended in a precarious equilibrium, calibrated between mouth and ear. What's more, this acoustic game goes beyond the adaptation of a voice to a listener to reveal a sonorization of thought, underscoring how much meaning depends on tone, volume, and timbre. And though it is possible to vary them, this does not just come from some strategy of communication, but more profoundly from a diversity internal to the speaker. An overly common idea would identify a person with the uniqueness of their voice, through recognition of its timbre. Nevertheless, each speaker, each thinker has many voices that derive as much from their physical characteristics as from their vocal education, from their culture, and from their mental investment in their speech. A voice can be controlled, but it sometimes escapes our will, for other voices are overlaid on the same voice. Different people speak at the same time, without the speaker always knowing who is speaking in and through them. Listening to these palimpsestuous and diffracted voices allows us to hear the diversity and the tensions that reign between the different selves who speak in the mouth of an "author."

4. Montaigne, *Essays*, 3.13, 834.

To think well is to hear well

The recognition of the sonic aspect of thought breaks with the ideality of speech that would depend on nothing but mind. The senses — in particular hearing — take part in the formation of ideas, just like affects and *entendement*, 'understanding' — a philosophical word that we forget also designates an intention toward sound. Few philosophers have accorded importance to acoustic questions, except for those melomaniacs who themselves played music. Among them, a few engaged passionately in musical disputes, like Rousseau, but rare were those who wondered about sound as sound, and rarer still were those who considered sound to be the main sense for thought. Without any doubt, the auditory turn in Western philosophy was incarnated by Nietzsche, though Nietzsche was certainly preceded by Schopenhauer who considered music to be a foundation of philosophical intuition. For Nietzsche, who boasted about having the smallest ears in the world, which is to say the most acute, the quality of someone's intelligence depended on their capacity to hear well. To think well, to read well, these required good listening. Instead of taking theoretical concepts and arguments literally, one needs to hear their scores, what keys they are in, their resonances. Nietzsche's famous metaphor, in which he defined himself as a philosopher with a hammer, has been read at face value, making him an idoloclast. Yet he himself identified this hammer as a *tuning fork*[5], and so as a tool that one strikes against an object to make its note sound and to verify the chords and discords it has with other sonic emissions. In English, more readily than in French, one can say sounds to indicate whether an idea sounds good or not. Nietzsche practiced systematic suspicion through his ears, always hearing

5. Friedrich Nietzsche, *Twilight of the Idols* (in *The Portable Nietzsche*, trans. Walter Kaufmann; Viking, 1968), 466.

something underneath, behind, or within, interrogating the voice of the subject speaking or writing. What we call Nietzsche's psychological readings of Socrates, Kant, or Hegel are above all a manner of listening, of putting his ear to their meaning and auscultating their theoretical claims, without allowing himself to be overawed by their univocal authority.

The philosophical as well as musical quarrels launched by Nietzsche can be understood through this attention to hearing. More than moral or aesthetic judgments, his denunciations of Platonic metaphysics or Wagnerian music rest on their sonic qualities: Socrates's voice resounded with a latent resentment toward reality, which he never stopped disdaining in favor of realms beyond; Wagner's tetralogy resonated in the ambitions of the Germanic Reich. Certainly, such precipitous judgments are provocations deserving of debate. Nevertheless, they are based on a second listening that is wary of explicit arguments in order to uncover, through their tonalities, their creators' motives, their secret scores. The subtle music of thought can be heard only on condition that one open one's ears and not be blinded by arguments from authority or appeals to universality.While Wagnerians might mock Nietzsche's preference for Bizet's Carmen, we must not forget that, beyond any musicological quarrel, sound remains primarily a matter of physiology and bodily health. Some sonic arrangements strike the nerves like poison, others enchant the mind, and it is up to the listener to determine which sonic dispositions — literary, philosophical, musical — are beneficial to them.

Nietzsche confided that all his thinking was guided by different musics, melodies, and sounds. Wagner, Schumann, and Chopin were sites of intellectual intensity, as much as were Heraclitus, Sophocles, and Stendhal. In *Ecce Homo*, when describing the maturation of his work *Thus Spoke Zarathustra*, which is a sort of symphonic poem, Nietzsche recalled a philosophical revelation that allowed him, during a walk in the Engadine, to conceive of the idea of the eternal return. Although commentators refer to this moment as his "vision" at Surlej, space and sight were less significant than sound, for Nietzsche emphasized the transformation of his hearing as generating this discovery, noting "a sudden and profoundly decisive change in my taste, especially in music."[6] He clarifies: "Perhaps the whole of *Zarathustra* may be reckoned as music; certainly a rebirth of the art of *hearing* was among its preconditions." The transformation described by Nietzsche goes far beyond a change of score or musical genre: It concerns the way one listens not only to music but also to the world. What's more, it engages a new way of writing and thinking with our ears. This auditory turn in philosophy would then be pursued by thinkers, such as Vladimir Jankélévitch and Clément Rosset, who, true to their Nietzschean inspiration, invested greatly in musicological and sonic stakes. Coming from other philosophical sources, thinkers like Wittgenstein or Adorno continued this idea that thinking is a matter of listening.

What does an "auditory turn in philosophy" mean? It would be illusory to believe that ideas have their own history, as though they exercised dominion over the reality of an age, when, on the contrary, they arise from it. That the question of sound arises at some moment of human history or other corresponds to changes in ways of listening and to developments in acoustic devices. The archaeology of thought allows us to describe these different evolutions, whether related to the construction of acoustic spaces in the theaters or political spaces of ancient Greece,

6. Friedrich Nietzsche, *Ecce Homo* (in *On the Genealogy of Morals* and *Ecce Homo*, trans. Walter Kaufmann; Vintage, 1969), 295.

to a particular art of conversation that developed in some sixteenth-century aristocratic societies, or to the invention of sonic devices like the gramophone, telephone, or tape recorder in the nineteenth and twentieth centuries, to which we will return. Upon discovering new sonic practices, certain philosophers tried their hands at new methods, like broadcasting or recording, that led them to discover theoretical stakes linked to sound. Whether or not they made this experimentation explicit, they came to take up new problems, or at least problems to which the history of philosophy had not paid as much attention. It was thus with Merleau-Ponty, whose reflections most known to us concern the gaze, the image, sight, and seeing, insofar as these were debated with Sartre or Lacan, and yet whose phenomenology also concerned listening and, more precisely, auditory consciousness.

Who do I hear when I speak?

There are some rather fascinating propositions on sound in Merleau-Ponty's *The Visible and the Invisible*, a posthumously published text to which he had consecrated the last years of his life from 1959 on. The audible earns its place in thinking on the visible, and not just by analogy. Straight away, Merleau-Ponty insists on the necessity of freeing speech from its language-based meanings in order to take up the relation of the vocal organ to thought. Speech welcomes thought not only thanks to the meaning of its words, but also through its resonance and participation in what Merleau-Ponty called the flesh of the world. "I am a sonic being,"[7] he wrote, which signifies that consciousness takes aim at the world through the sounds it emits and through

7. Merleau-Ponty, *The Visible and the Invisible* (trans. Alphonso Lingis; Northwestern University Press, 1968), 144. Translation modified: Lingis used "sonorous being" rather than "sonic being" for *être sonore.*

those it receives. Nevertheless, Merleau-Ponty's interrogation is more precisely about the reflexive phenomenon of listening: What does it mean to hear yourself speak? "I hear my own vibration from within," he observed. The speech of a speaking being returns from without and from within; it thus makes that speaking being experience what the movement of a voice is, extended toward others but also manifesting a body that is present to the world through this faculty of speech.

There is no unitary voice unique to the subject. Rather than presupposing an objectively identifiable voice for each speaker, a particular voice that would sign for the univocal subject's intention, Merleau-Ponty was interested in the phenomenon of speech as it arises from the emergent voice he called *vociferation*: "There is a reflexivity of the movements of phonation and of hearing; they have their sonic inscription, the vociferations have in me their motor echo."[8] Experiencing oneself as a sonic being leads thus to understanding that speaking and conversing are not reducible to exchanging words, ideas, and meanings. These actions take part in the manifestation of the world as a soundscape, the speaking body participating in the vibration of all beings.

> Freeing voice as vociferation from signifying intention, Merleau-Ponty radically modified the approach to listening: The meaning of words only exists though their incarnation in a voice and, reversibly, a voice makes each person conscious of their sonic being and their inscription in a language. Consequently, to understand a phrase is nothing else than to fully welcome it in its sonic being, or, as we put it so well, to *hear what it says* (*l'entendre*). The meaning is not on the phrase like the butter on the bread, like a second layer of 'psychic reality' spread over

8. *Ibid.*

> the sound: it is the totality of what is said, the integral of all the differentiations of the verbal chain; it is given with the words for those who have ears to hear.[9]

Listening to other people's sentences in their sonic texture, hearing oneself as vociferation and vibration — these attitudes modify the relations sentences have to speech and even to meaning. That a philosopher like Merleau-Ponty, who had devoted himself above all to the gaze and to touch, was capable of such auditory attention bears witness to the mid-twentieth-century eruption of questions about listening into philosophical reflection, which had historically always accorded prominence to sight. The auditory turn in philosophy is thus that our contemporary ear is sensitive to these questions of listening, whether they come from Renaissance thinkers and their reform of the know-how of hearing (*savoir-entendre*), from the Nietzschean revolution in the art of philosophical listening, or from a phenomenology of the speaking and listening body. If our interest in sound can develop at moments where the acoustics of our lives change with modern technology, this should also apply to the sonic worlds of old. In particular, we can "turn" our auricles differently in order to capture waves of sound that have escaped us till now and to direct our radar toward new sonic worlds, even if they were already being emitted around us and within us.

9. *Ibid.*, 155. Translation modified.

III. Thinking with an Accent?

If we admit that a thought has to be listened to and that sounds are carriers of meaning, it becomes important to analyze audible phenomena concretely, not only orally, but in writing. To avoid having sound fall back on meaning and only hearing a word according to its rhetorical effects, we become interested in features of sound that appear minor or unimportant. Accent is one such feature. Rarely the object of theoretical study, accent is considered superficial, even though it implies any number of linguistic, social, or psychological stakes. Subtle analysis of accent requires deciphering numerous characteristics that are not reducible to phonetics: the delivery of speech, its rhythms and velocities; ways of articulating; intonations; volumes; stresses; inflections; modulations; etc. A strictly analytic and linguistic approach to accent, however, does not suffice to understand its psychological and intellectual functions.

Accent is something others have

Attending to accent is of interest to sonic thought if we hear *accent* in terms of *accentuation*, which is to say in terms of a speaker's positioning with respect to language. To accentuate entails following rules of enunciation that require placing a stronger or weaker stress (*accent*) on certain syllables. But it also implies a personalization of speech, an often unconscious disposition to "speak like" one's linguistic milieu. One's accent is regional and stems from a collective determination, since it comes from speech patterns of a group becoming embedded in the very voice of the language learner. The illusory naturalness of accent even leads speakers to believe they are "accentless," all the while detecting accents in those who speak differently, thereby betraying their belonging to foreign soil. A Béarnais, a Parisian, a Belgian, or a Québécois will each spontaneously spot the others' different ways of speaking French, without being aware that the same could be done for them. The identification of other peoples' accents — *accent is something others have!* — takes on any number of distinctions and hierarchies according to nationality, ethnicity, gender, or social status. The relation of speakers to their ways of speaking, however, is not just about following usage rules, but entails a rather rich psychological investment.

A speaker's subjectivization manifests in particular when they must express themselves in a foreign language. As is often the case, it is when we adopt the point of view of foreignness, of non-naturalness, that we discover what we had ceased to hear due to habit. With a new language, we must incorporate new phonemes, new accentuations, and unhabitual ways of breathing. This effort calls into question a subject's attachment to their so-called maternal or native language. Keeping or losing an accent goes beyond one's auditory abilities and involves, to a greater degree, psychological attitudes of resistance to new accentuations. How else are we to explain that certain speakers, though living for decades in a foreign country and having mastered its language, still have a strong accent while others can get their accents to almost disappear? One avenue of explanation is in the relation certain thinkers have to their voice and their accent, especially when they experience a divergence between their internal speech and the conventional norm. Such dissonance has been commented on by Jacques Derrida, Pierre Bourdieu, Édouard Glissant, and Zadie Smith in terms of their so-called regional accents, as well as by Julia Kristeva in her transition from Bulgarian to French. We shall try to hear how this dissonance appears not only orally, but in writing.

Is accent perceptible in thought? Such a question seems absurd, or we understand it only metaphorically, with accent as the echo of an origin. And yet, it is indeed in the concrete sounds of accent that we can link accent to the writing of thought, to the search for a tone that accords with thought or suppresses it. Active through its effects or its repression, accent should be studied in and of itself. Derrida talks about accent in a digression during some reflections on language, and his personal testimony uncovers previously unheard sonic stakes for philosophy. His remarks took shape during a debate on multilingualism with Édouard Glissant and Abdelkebir Khatibi at Baton Rouge in 1992. Khatibi, a Moroccan sociologist, had written books on bilingualism, and Glissant, a poet from Martinique, had undertaken a lengthy reflection on language creolization. In their presence, Derrida interrogated the notion of "maternal" language and shared his colonial experience where different vernaculars intertwined. During his childhood in Algeria, he became familiar with French, Arabic, Berber, and Hebrew. He thus maintained an ambiguous relation to the French language, one that saw both academic success and colonial domination, as when he suffered exclusion from school during the war for being Jewish. In developing his mediation on the impurity and impropriety of any idiom, Derrida proclaims his proximity to Glissant's theses on the ambivalent relation to French felt by those who acquired it through domestication and who hear many languages when they speak or write it. These three interlocutors showcase a way of speaking French with accents that resonate in proximity to other dialects, accents that are forms of resistance to the dominant speech norm and to the supposedly neutral standard accent.

Writing to no longer hear yourself
The paradox of this resistance to linguistic domestication, shown by creoles and regional accents, arises from the combination of the manner in which a speaker adopts a language said to be "proper" to a nation, their fascination with its prestige, and their alienation in believing that it gives access to the universal. A speaker's repression of their local accent or dialect disdained as a patois contributes to their supposed emancipation for, by taming their voice, they break free of their particular determinations and gain access to the town hall — *la maison commune*, literally 'the shared home' — such is the meaning of domestication, of the *domus*. And yet, the best way to erase a speaker's regional accent is to write, for writing is thought to be accentless. All while being silent, writing imposes an atonic syntax and institutes a standard grammar with its system of implicit values. For writers who wished to erase their regional ways of speaking, written language gives cover: It covers over their original voice, masking the inner, corporeal work of language and its private imaginings.

In France in particular, the suppression of regional languages through schooling during the Third Republic created suspicion about their persistence in the form of accents. Pierre Bourdieu had analyzed the stakes of social positioning linked to the *habitus*, which included clothing, cultural tastes concerning "distinction," and accent. On a more personal note, in his *Sketch for a Self-Analysis*, Bourdieu evoked his Béarnais childhood living in the countryside and recalled the bullying he experienced very early on due to his accent when one of his classmates, who had himself taken on a "corrected accent," mocked his pronunciation: He "often tormented me by pronouncing my name in the manner of the peasants of the region and joking about the name of my village, which symbolized all peasant backwardness."[1] All the more so when he arrived in Paris where he discovered that such differentiation was even more pronounced between well-born adolescents and the rest, and he confesses having worked on erasing his Béarnais accent during his entry to the École Normale Supérieure.

"Correcting" one's accent is a notion that implies both the idea of a norm and, with it, the necessity of correction, even punishment. In French, the word *correct* makes us hear idioms like *prendre une correction*, 'to be punished', or *maison de correction*, 'juvenile detention center', based on its polysemy of justice and direction. In fact, until the middle of the twentieth century, children who spoke creole at school got their fingers rapped with a cane, as did those who continued to communicate using some regional language in the metropole. But for all that, is an original accent forgotten once it's "corrected"? Is it kept unconsciously? Does it remain on the tongue? And can others hear it despite all efforts at correction? Such questions haunt speakers forced to correct their ways of speaking by being subject to a dominant linguistic superego and anxious about entering into a community of speakers. Accents are indeed not reducible to manners of speaking, to phonetic characteristics. Above all, they also create soundscapes that are at once natural and cultural.

Where language and accent differ, we find a separation between place of origin and new world that corresponds to a rupture in continuity between landscapes. So it was for an Algerian Jew like Derrida or a Martinican like Glissant in their discovery of different climates,[2] flora, and sounds,

1. Pierre Bourdieu, *Sketch for a Self-Analysis* (trans. Richard Nice; Polity, 2007), 98.
2. See Glissant's discovery of snow: Édouard Glissant, *Sun of Consciousness* (trans. Nathanaël; Nightboat Books, 2020), 18.

whether sounds of the physical environment or those of language. Speaking or reading in a language while adopting its sonic norms leads to a change in listening and pronunciation. "One entered French literature only by losing one's accent,"[3] declared Derrida. And yet, what does "losing one's accent" mean when reading a text? Does such reading imply taking on the presumed accent of the author? Do the words and sentences of French literature require a different accent or even the absence of any accent? And yet a good number of accents, fictional or not, can be heard in old texts, as in the Picard, Norman, or Occitan accents of many medieval texts. And perhaps a little Provençal can be detected in the works of Marcel Pagnol or Jean Giono. The task of losing one's own accent seems primarily linked to the interiorization of some original shame, which must be expiated by "correction" and a willed deafness to language through neutralization.

Jackie Derrida had an accent that (got) killed

Philosophy, more than literature, is supposed to have no accent; resorting to abstraction, it does not allow any particular voice to be heard. Such a statement, to be sure, should be nuanced by citing philosophical writings that assume their soundscapes, notably those of Rousseau. Still, if we fall back on the majority conceptual practice, philosophical language seems to eradicate any accent. This is why it offers one of the better resorts to speakers who want to silence whatever reflects their particular origin. The language of science, even more than that of philosophy, has been the linguistic refuge for speakers who seek to integrate into the culture of native speakers: Many "vocations" for science have been born in the mutism and anonymity of

3. Jacques Derrida, *Monolingualism of the Other* (trans. Patrick Mensah, Stanford University Press, 1998), 45.

its language. "I would like to hope, I would very much prefer, that no publication permit my Algerian 'French' to appear,"[4] wrote Derrida, thus supposing that writing would make his intonation, as a marker of his belonging to a non-native soundscape, disappear. Such suppression in the form of self-censoring one's origins is not just exerted against the self or limited to a matter of psychology: It reinstates and reaffirms, socially and politically, a hierarchy of accents and language practices.

There exist good and bad accents for philosophical speech and writing, the good accent being the one that is not heard, that makes itself inconspicuous behind the universal. Derrida confides:

> An accent — any French accent, but above all a strong southern accent — seems incompatible to me with the intellectual dignity of public speech. (Unacceptable, no? Well, I admit it.) Incompatible, a fortiori, with the vocation of poetic speech: For example, when I heard René Char read his solemn aphorisms with an accent that struck me as at once comical and obscene, as the betrayal of a truth, it ruined, in no small measure, an admiration of my youth.[5]

Derrida, who had deconstructed so much of what he called phallogocentrism — the purity of literal meaning, pretentions to the universal — this same philosopher, despite himself, takes up the discrimination of accents. Accepting his own alienation, he falls back on the idea of a model of unaccented speech that would invalidate speech in which distinctive features could be heard and that would judge its source as unworthy of bearing philosophy or poetry. What Derrida calls the betrayal of a truth,

4. *Ibid.*, 45–46. Translation modified.
5. *Ibid.*, 46. Translation modified.

indicating a corruption of the universal, comes rather from the revelation of the speaker's origin, who is betrayed by their accent, laid bare, and then mocked for this obscenity. The presence of an accent exposes the homeland and community to which the speaker belongs, while its absence would allow the speaker to remain in the heaven of ideas. To be sure, Derrida's oeuvre began with a questioning of orality in writing; nevertheless, the admission of his value judgments regarding accent reflects first and foremost his relation to theoretical language, which attempts to erase original ways of speaking.

Such an imperative to kill one's accent to achieve so-called neutral speech is frequently interiorized by speakers who live in a position of exteriority regarding language. Atavistic speakers, those who do not feel that their way of speaking reveals foreignness, assume their accents more willingly. Such was the case for Gaston Bachelard, who serves as a counterexample to what Bourdieu had maintained, for he did not at all seek to suppress his strong Burgundian accent, even when teaching epistemology. Doubtless Bachelard did not see his accent as downgrading him socially or ethnically. On the other hand, immigrant speakers are marked by their accent and designated *francophone* — a discriminatory qualification negatively identifying those who are not from France's mainland. More than others these writers experience speech norms and correction. Some of them become "more royalist than the king" and more censorious than the keepers of the standard idiom. Social integration takes place, in effect, at the price of overvaluing linguistic mastery: Particularly in France, speaking good French is the price to be paid to become a good citizen. The work of constraining one's voice and corseting one's pronunciation are described by Derrida as the construction of a dam or lock to retain his accent's surging volume and rhythm: "This dam is always threatening to give way. I was the first to be afraid of my own voice, as if it were not mine, and to contest it, even to detest it."[6] Glissant too feared his own voice, which he thought was high-pitched, and he was also conscious of moderating his accent according to whether he was speaking in public or in private. We should document all those writers and thinkers who didn't like their voice, who experienced unease at having it heard in public, and who worked to normalize it. Beckett, phobic to audio recordings, would figure among the most obsessional.

English speakers too, in their relation to the language of the Empire, find themselves in a war of accents, as the writer Zadie Smith remarkably showed in her novels and in a lecture given at the New York Public Library in 2008 titled "Speaking in Tongues." In that lecture she spoke of her voice, which had become so different from that of her childhood, and of her experience of being split in two upon adopting a British way of speaking that was closer to Cambridge than to the diverse, working-class neighborhoods of London where she grew up. Accent, she observed, seemed everywhere to be a marker of class membership or ethnicity. And yet, when she shifts her attention to the ways in which the then newly elected American president Barack Obama spoke, she notes his astonishing capacity to take on different accents, each characteristic of rather different milieus, when addressing different populations. She detects in this an aptitude for adopting many voices to the point of no longer needing to be attached to a single voice of his own, even his original voice. "Having more than one voice in your ear is not a burden, or not solely a

6. *Ibid.*, 48. Translation modified.

burden — it is also a gift."[7] Doubtless such freedom to circulate among accents is more often shared by speakers who readily assume a multiplicity of the self, which stems from what one might call mixed ethnicity. *Being many-voiced* suggests, in any event, whatever the social conditioning may be, that there exist many voices in each person and that the way a person speaks with an accent has to do with complex and stratified relations to their affiliations.

These reflections on accent and the multiplicity of voices make us hear just how much every thought is prone to intonation, whether it stems from some code or from psycholinguistic torsions. They contradict the ideal of an atonic philosophical writing, this fantasy of the *silenced accent*[8] that has been handed down by any number of philosophers since antiquity, imposing on us a deafness to their vernaculars. The illusion of a theoretical writing without grain, without body, without unique voice, arises from trying to find phrasings without tonality, which would be phrasings for the anonymous universal. Nevertheless, the act of speaking or writing requires that we find an intonation for it. The choice of tone engages, in effect, the very spirit of philosophy, whether it be the "tone of superiority" identified by Kant, or an apocalyptic or bellicose tone.[9] More generally, the history of philosophy bears witness to the fact that language itself entails a range of tones and modes of theoretical exposition. Consider those thinkers who opted for ordinary rather than learned language, like

7. Zadie Smith, "Speaking in Tongues" (in *The Best American Essays 2010*, ed. Christopher Hitchens; Mariner Books, 2010), 183.
8. Translator's note: The original *accent tué*, here as 'silenced accent' in the sense of being, more literally, 'the killed(-off) accent', also echoes its opposites *accentué*, 'accented' or 'accentuated', and *un accent qui tue*, 'a rather strong accent' (literally 'an accent that kills'). This section's title in French is *L'accent tué de Jackie Derrida.*
9. See Pierre Bouretz, *D'un ton guerrier en philosophie : Habermas, Derrida & Co* (Gallimard, 2011).

Montaigne who found a new way of philosophizing in French rather than in Latin, or Descartes who resorted to this "vulgar" tongue to set forth his method. Adopting a particular language for writing and putting into it intonations that are ironic, or erudite, or rustic — choices like these determine thought, which is never dissociable from the way it is worded.

Writing with an accent

It remains difficult to identify in some piece of writing what, beyond its tone, pertains to accent. And yet, Derrida holds that the "symptomatology" of accent nevertheless "invades writing."[10] Linguists have identified orthographies, signs, and turns of phrase that can make the oral audible in writing, but we must not confuse the oral as transcribed into writing and "oral writing." The way in which a piece of writing produces an intonation or an accent is an operation of writing. In this way, the phonetic transcription of, say, a rustic way of speaking — like the one Molière gave to the peasants in his *Dom Juan* — has nothing in common with an oralized writing like that of Céline in *Journey to the End of the Night*. No doubt we should understand "accent" differently, especially in texts that are not *meant* to be listened to, like philosophical writings with their "abstract" language from which regional particularities have been eliminated. Quite similar to the question of gender and the inquiry into a writing that would be *women*'s writing (écriture *féminine*), the question of accent must be approached via detours, without seeking direct phonetic transcription. What, then, should we lend our ears to?

10. Derrida, *Monolingualism of the Other*, 46.

To hear an accent or some accentuation within writing, we must first distinguish the physical voice of the writer and their "voice" in writing. For it would be naive to believe that a novelist or philosopher with a Provençal accent must produce Provençal-sounding works! Derrida's disappointment listening to René Char precisely underscores this distinction between, on the one hand, a poetic, written, sonic language and, on the other, a physical voice. Nevertheless, there exists an indirect link between the two. Roland Barthes proposed the notion of *grain* in an attempt to make the corporeal dimension of song or writing audible. Enunciation, when written down, is not unrelated to the speaker's vocalization, their rhymes, phrasings, or accents. As Barthes makes clear: "The 'grain' is the body in the voice as it sings, the hand as it writes, the limb as it performs."[11] The idea of a *body of thought* is not reducible to a metaphor, and it is in this corporeal grain that sound gets released, with its breaths and rhythms and their transformation in the heart of written language. As we observed with oral accent, the psychological dimensions of an accent in writing can be heard all the more clearly when a writer changes their language.

To write, speak, or think in a foreign language radically alters the body's dispositions and ways of expressing itself; it makes us hear the particularly corporeal aspect of a voice through its accents, which, in a less familiar language, resonate more loudly. Against their will, a speaker lets old sounds resound, though they thought they had lost them in their ways of pronouncing and thinking in this new language. Julia Kristeva attests to this with the persistence of her native Bulgarian in her use of French, which she nonetheless mastered better than many native speakers:

11. Roland Barthes, "The Grain of the Voice" (in *Image — Music — Text*, trans. Stephen Heath; Hill and Wang, 1977), 188.

> You improve your ability with another instrument, as one expresses oneself with algebra or the violin. You can become a virtuoso with this new device that moreover gives you a new body, just as artificial and sublimated — some say sublime. You have a feeling that the new language is a resurrection: new skin, new sex. But the illusion bursts when you hear, upon listening to a recording, for instance, that the melody of your voice comes back to you as a peculiar sound, out of nowhere, closer to the old spluttering than to today's code.[12]

In a foreign language, the body takes on new accents, strikes its syllables differently, and breathes. Nevertheless, Kristeva, a psychoanalyst, hears in this an actor's performance that does not engage the speaker's unconscious. A foreign or second language seems artificial to her, like playing a character role, compared to one that might be more "natural" or closer to her first language. Despite Kristeva's reservations, we nevertheless observe that expressing ourselves in a language other than one's "mother" tongue allows us to experience a different speaking and desiring body: Inhibitions associated with the acquisition of language during our childhood disappear, and this new way of expressing ourselves enables acts of boldness tied to a sense of play that are as intellectual as they are sexual. Performance is not reducible to some temporary illusion, at a remove from our drives; it is the vector for another self, a multiple self that requisitions old accents and repressions and gives them a new outlet: a mouth and a tongue that move differently, vocal cords that vibrate differently, lungs that regulate air in a new way, and altered gestures that accompany phonation. The whole body is put on notice for new accentuation.

12. Julia Kristeva, *Strangers to Ourselves* (trans. Leon S. Roudiez; Columbia University Press, 1991), 15.

That the truth of the body resides in the so-called mother tongue is not necessarily an idea accepted by all bilingual or multilingual speakers and writers. Some acquire several languages simultaneously in childhood and use them according to the parent or relative they are speaking to. Such relatives may be living in exile or in a multilingual society. Polyglotism would then attest less to a fracturing of the self than to its multiplicity. It is not language in itself, but speaking to others that mobilizes a speaker's identities with their fluctuating accentuations. In a subtle way, accent involves the speaking body in a relation of in-betweenness that unites it with the body being spoken to, marking its difference or trying to speak like it. All those in exile know the desire to be heard to some degree, and so the refusal to dilute their vocal singularity in the other's sonic world. Writers have shown these movements from one milieu to another through languages and accents. Some allow the accents of other languages to be heard in the one they chose, while others translate themselves and play with the typical sounds of each language. "I write in the presence of all the world's languages," Glissant claimed when asked how he defined being a francophone writer.

> When I write, I hear all these languages, even those I don't understand, simply out of kinship. This is a new fact of contemporary literature and of current sensibilities: We create our language from the many languages that are available to us through immersion or through television, lectures, world music, whether Icelandic sagas or African songs. These languages are in our language not as nonsense but as a profound, and perhaps hidden, presence.[13]

13. Édouard Glissant, interview with Lila Azam Zanganeh, *Le Monde*, 3 February 2011.

It is thus not just creole that we can hear in Glissant's writing, as a Martiniquan who chose to write in French, but many other languages as well through the undefinable company he kept with them.

The question of accent is thus multiplied, both externally and internally. Externally, multilingualism brings languages into contact and transforms them, as evidenced by permeable writings, like those that creolize English and Spanish in New York, Florida, or California. Internally, Glissant's suggestion targets the very composition of each language, constituted and traversed by dialects and diverse sources that we do not always hear. Multiple accents can thus be grafted onto pieces of writing, not only because of national affiliations but also through encounters and affinities. Many francophone writers find themselves in a position to shift accents from one language to another, because they are writing in the presence of residual, repressed, or reduced sounds. Their writings in French work on the differences and deviations in accentuations and rhythms that mark their speaking bodies, which come from countries or childhoods now lost to move among languages whose accents they modulate and transform. These movements appear even more clearly when the same writer uses multiple languages. The best examples here are bilingual authors, who allow us to hear this circulation of accents and their usefulness in traversing the imaginaries and sounds of writing. Kafka, Pessoa, Nabokov, or Beckett continuously composed by working on the gaps between the languages they used, and their texts are populated with echoes between these different sonic environments. To hear accents in a text and in thought thus implies listening to these reverberations, which are not reducible to phonetic features: A piece of writing, whether of fiction or of theory, establishes soundscapes and sets out on a journey from one body and one culture to another, which we can perceive in phenomena as slight and powerful as an accent, a breath, a shout, or a whisper.

IV. Screams and Suffocations

Recent work on the voices of philosophers, like Gilles Deleuze, Jacques Lacan, and Michel Foucault, thanks to recordings of their seminars, has opened up new areas for study. These recordings allow us to hear the corporeal vocalities and soundscapes that breathe life into their arguments and ideas. Thought indeed comprises reasons, affects, corporealities, etc., and their interlacing is perceptible in the voice that carries them. This claim seems obvious when listening to speech, but less so when reading texts. The challenge of such an *auscultation* of writing is to bring to light this repressed sonic substrate in order to read texts with one's ears. Concretely, this undertaking begins with the most minimal element of vocalization, breath, without which no speech is possible. To understand how thinkers breathe life into their arguments, we must start from their breath.

How can we hear breath again in language? The notion of breath must first be relieved of an old metaphorical burden that keeps us from approaching it clearly and distinctly. The extra meanings and images linked to breath appeared quite early, in the very first texts on language. At issue there was a particular type of air, the *pneuma*, in which Greek thinkers, above all the Stoics, placed the soul. More than physical or acoustic, this air is metaphysical, for it immediately confers a meaning on speech that goes beyond it. Unlike the cries or songs of birds, human breath is assumed to be destined for speech and is manifest in the voice. Its meaning comes from elsewhere, not only through its content, but above all thanks to the very essence of speaking: its vocation to intelligibility. A close reading of texts from antiquity would, of course, lead us to nuance this distinction, which has become too simplistic. Aristotle, for example, starting from a physics of air, maintains that human and non-human animals have a "voice."[1] And yet, the philosophical metaphor became established primarily with the word *inspiration*, the fortunes of which would carry across the centuries. By its etymology, *spirare*, inspiration associates breath and spirit, whether of God or of an idea. A metaphysical border is thus set up to distinguish, on the one hand, air that is breathed in, entering from the outside (the sky, the ether, the ideal, etc.) and penetrating all the way to the inner soul, and, on the other hand, physical air as the mere agitation of atoms produced by exhalation, limited to the collision of molecular masses and currents of air. The former produces thought and carries meaning, whereas the latter remains a bodily, soul-less deed, as for those animal-machines described by Descartes and Malebranche whose cries simply come from the flow of air in their pipes. Far from such a distinction, hearing breath in human speech in concrete terms requires obviating this metaphysical memory and its dualism separating good air from bad, the inspired from the insane, the human from the animal.

Linguistics, being more focused on acoustics, has freed itself from notions of inspiration, but only to establish yet again a distinction that governs the concept of breath: articulated versus unarticulated or inarticulate. Linguistics indeed relies on the principle of articulation to establish the specificity of human speech. Air exhaled by the lungs produces sounds through contractive movements of the speech organs, like the tongue or lips. The term *articulation* — already used by Rousseau in his reflections on language — was taken up by linguists, but also by

1. See the analysis by Sarah Kay of Aristotle's treatise *On the Soul* in her "Circulating Air: Inspiration, Voice and Soul in Poetry and Song," Paragraph 41.1 (*Soundings and Soundscapes*, eds. Sarah Kay and Francois Noudelmann, Edinburgh University Press, 2018), 10–25.

psychoanalysts to observe how children construct meaning or invest psychologically in certain phonemes. What interest, then, could there be in what remains unarticulated, in that formless part of breath prior to phonation? Preverbal, animalistic, regressive ... the inarticulate, by definition, only exists by default: it is not articulated. What more is there to say? Its utterance, its breath, whether scream or suffocation, lacks meaning; it stays in the forest with the wild child, or in the dereliction of the mute or screaming madman. Such breath without distinction gains no credit, but is once again relegated to the realm of the animal, nature, or noise. Unless, that is, we hear its acoustics differently and resist the metaphors of metaphysics. What is called inarticulate might harbor thought and might not be limited to what is indistinct. One writer, speaker, and screamer undertook this reversal, sometimes at the risk of madness: Artaud, who thus proposed, in his thinking and his practice, to radically upset the privilege European culture accorded to what is verbal or articulated. Artaud brought breath and its physics back to the theater of language and put it frontstage.

Breath before the syllable

The preverbal arouses a good number of fantasies in writers and artists who have sought a primitive, wild place among the uncivilized or the refractory, in order to free themselves from cultural norms. Still, this interest in a realm beyond words, whether as transgressive utopia or methodological hypothesis, puts the overwhelming power of articulated language at a distance, allowing one to explore phenomena linked to breath and to hear their meanings. In a 1932 letter of incredible power to Jean Paulhan, Artaud outlined a project for a new language that would rediscover the moment of primal utterance and maintain the link between the body and its psyche. Artaud thereby performed a return to physical breath as constitutive of thought, without dissociating body and psyche. This moment he calls "gesture," which reunites "its material and its wits."[2] For articulation divides — such is its flaw. Though certainly necessary to create distinct units and to impel a rhythm, articulation separates the body from language, making it an autonomous system. Artaud's ambition was part of the revolution of artistic avant-gardes aimed at overturning the history of European art — its treatment of language, particularly in theater — in order to invent a different grammar, one founded on gesture more than on speech. Seeking other sources, he believed that he had found a model for this new theater in Balinese traditions. Artaud's thinking, however, goes beyond an avant-garde rhetoric destructive of European culture. It is more than an indictment of rationality, in the manner of surrealist provocations, but goes to the point of origin of all expression, prior to articulation, where the physical and the mental mingle. He brings to mind the repressed in language and leads us to listen to what constitutes it, at the very heart of the speaking and thinking voice.

In Artaud's letter, which showcases the power of breath through words and gestures, his project seems to be the rewriting of the history of language, attempting to locate its prehistory in order to rediscover the path that leads to speech. For articulated language did not develop according to some destiny of human nature; it was not born on its own, but carries other materialities besides verbal signs. An alternative history must therefore set itself to listening to the sedimentations that led to the pronunciation of syllables. Artaud announced a radical proposal: His new

2. Antonin Artaud, *The Theater and Its Double* (trans. Mary Caroline Richards; Grove Press, 1958), 110.

grammar would bring "again into the light all the relations fixed and enclosed in the strata of the human syllable, which has killed them by confining them."[3] Rather than unfurling our faculty of speech and allowing for the evolution of language, the syllable eliminated the relations that this verbal language had to its initial materialities, to those gestures that existed prior to linguistic articulation. Such a suggestion is revolutionary. It suggests that the relations between word and body are not ones of articulation, but of inclusion and grafting. After such an overturning, the task would be to recover these operations of knotting, these forgotten interlacings, that have been repressed by the linguistic and symbolic order. Nietzsche, in his demystification of the concept, had already performed such a reversal by recalling the role of the corporeal, the sensible, the affective, and the imaginary in the language of rationality. He decrypted the abstract language of philosophy as a strategy to evacuate the sensible from it (out of either a hatred for the real or an inability to live it), and thus he rewrote the history of Western rationality, from the Platonic *logos* to Kantian schematism and Hegelian universalism. The concept, supposed to unify the diversity of sensation, reveals itself to be the product of metaphors that it conceals yet which continue to act clandestinely. Taking up this Nietzschean gesture, Artaud sought "a point still deeper, more remote from thought."[4] Like a discoverer of sounds, he captured cries, onomatopoeias, physical signs, "nervous modulations,"[5] which remain in articulated language and thought but which have been relegated as insignificant and inaudible, whence his desire to make them audible again.

3. *Ibid.*
4. *Ibid.*
5. *Ibid.*Translation modified.

Rediscovering the breath of thought thus no longer means seeking metaphysical inspiration, but physically listening to the bodily part of meaning. Artaud had the ambition of providing a space for this breath, and he imagined drama that would be the inverse of traditional French theater and the superiority it bestowed on the word over the body for expressing passions and ideas. Against character psychology, against articulated speech that transforms the movements of even the most archaic psyche into objective words, he offered a different stage, one that was plastic and sonic. Speech would no longer be a verbal instrument that translated feelings, but would rediscover the way it circulated through its bodily organs and its environment. Artaud wanted to materialize it, redirect it, and throw its breath back into the flux of the stage:

> To change the role of speech in theater is to make use of it in a concrete and spatial sense, combining it with everything in the theater that is spatial and significant in the concrete domain; to manipulate it like a solid object, one which overturns and disturbs things, in the air first of all, then in an infinitely more mysterious and secret domain.[6]

On this condition, then, language would no longer be limited to expressing or articulating thought, for it would be thought itself.

Cries of thought

How are we to listen to this physical breath of thought? Artaud mobilized it in the cry or scream through which he discerned a truth of the thinking body:

6. *Ibid.*, 72.

> Now there are in the human breath sudden shifts and breaks in tone and, from one scream to another, abrupt transferences by which the openings and soarings of the entire body of things can be suddenly evoked, which can support or liquify an organ like a tree you might prop up against the massy mountain of its forest.[7]

Far from being the primal unleashing of an objectless drive, the scream is an operation that mobilizes the history of language, rediscovers its source, and reactivates the relations speech has to the elements that coexist with it. In the radio play he wrote in 1948, *To Have Done With The Judgment of God*, Artaud introduces screams, vocalizations, and glossolalias, which he blends with the sounds of various instruments.[8] He thereby denounced the asphyxiation of language and fought against his own suffocation, which he countered with explosions of breath in quantity. Poetry and theater then rediscover the aerial and expansive power of language.

In philosophy, too, we can hear cries and screams, not only in references to real cries, but also in writing itself. In his seminar on Spinoza and the speeds of thought, Deleuze locates moments where cries can be heard in certain passages of the *Ethics*.[9] Unexpectedly, he points out

7. Antonin Artaud, "Theater and Science" (in *Artaud Anthology*, ed. Jack Hirschman, trans. Daniel Moore; City Lights Books, 1965), 171–72.
8. Evelyne Grossman, in her introduction to this play, suggests that Artaud understood the word radio *broadcast* (*émission*) in the sense of the production of sounds and waves, but also in an organic sense of an emission of screams, spit, saliva, sperm, farts, blood, excrement, etc. See *Pour en finir avec le jugement de Dieu* (in Antonin Artaud, *Œuvres*; Gallimard, 2004), 1636.
9. Gilles Deleuze, Seminar on Spinoza, 2 December 1980: "There are cries that come out of Spinoza. This is even more interesting since, again, this philosopher, who passes for an image of serenity, it's curious, when does he start shouting? He cries out a lot actually in the Scholia." http://www2.univ-paris8.fr/deleuze/article.php3?id_article=91

vociferations and times where Spinoza, whom tradition associates with serenity, gets carried away with ideas. Deleuze's remarks go well beyond stylistic analysis, for they underline the essential link between the form and content of thought. In this case, he observes, Spinoza is one of those philosophers who takes the body seriously. Deleuze discovered this same presence of basic cries in the work of Nietzsche, who also kept any pondering about the soul at a distance in order to express his interest in the powers of the body. And Deleuze employed the expression *cris de la pensée*, 'cries of thought', judging that a concept can also be heard as a cry. This proposal to hear breath at work at the heart of a piece of theoretical writing opens up a new field of study interested in the bodily, sonic dimension of language. And doubtless we should not limit the force of cries to those philosophers who rehabilitated the body, for in any thought, even the most abstract, there are breaths and pronouncements circulating. Concepts themselves are often cries emitted from a vital, nervous necessity that focuses on just one word.

Cries of thought come from the investment thinkers have in their pet words. They scream their lungs out, they bellow, they whisper, and they breathe out the notions that circulate through their writings. Under what condition can we say that a text is animated by one or more cries? At the most basic level, we can identify cries that get reported in texts. Simone Weil, for example, frequently mentions cries related to birth, hunger, pain, or existential doubt. Faced with God's silence, she wrote: "To cry like this throughout our brief and interminable, interminable and brief sojourn in this world, and then disappear into nothingness — it is enough."[10] Nevertheless, can we say not only

10. Simone Weil, *First and Last Notebooks* (trans. Richard Rees; Wipf & Stock, 1970), 137.

that certain texts are populated by noises, but that they themselves make noise? Expressions like "this text is a cry out to humanity" remain at the level of metaphor. But it's certainly the case that many works proceed from a revolt against tragic or emotional situations in ways we could call a cry. The word *éCRIture*, 'writing', with *CRI*, 'CRY', capitalized, has been used to refer to texts directly inspired by transgressive passions.[11] Still, referring to affects like a feeling of horror in the face of cruelty does not guarantee that we can identify a common inspiration for the "cry," which is a word that embraces distinct realities. Its force or coherence comes only from the affective and political images, values, and representations associated with it. We should resist these agglomerations of meaning and ask simply: Is a cry always "wild"? Do all cries resonate in the same way? Is a cry not first of all a word, nothing but a word onto which fantasies and affects are grafted? The word *cry*, in its brevity, sounds like an onomatopoeia, but it comes from a verb, an articulated verb with a Latin etymon, *quiritare*, which means to call upon citizens to give aid and to protest. If returning to a breath that is prior to the syllable allows us to hear the meaning of words differently, corporeally, then the cry does not get reduced to a purely emotive breath. It composes complex verbal and sonic environments. The breath cried out, to be properly heard, must be perceived as a compositional force. Put another way, a cry is never alone; it makes itself heard in composition.

As we suggested for breath, we must get rid of an "expressive" understanding of the cry in which cries would always arise from passion and trauma. There is indeed a mythology — or phantasm — concerning the cry so

11. Alain Marc has proposed to identify cry writings and to trace their genealogy from Sade to Pierre Guyotat. See Alain Marc, *Écrire le cri* (L'Écarlate, 2000).

onerous that it keeps us from taking up that which is unarticulated or inarticulate without ascribing weighty meanings to it. The challenge to language by artistic avant-gardes has doubtless contributed to this overflow of meaning: In opposition to the articulated, the code, the norm, or power, the cry is supposed to come from authentic depths, from a primal source presumed pristine and unsocialized. A fascination with raw and asocial utterances brings together a chain of images in which the primordial, the natural, and the corporeal are mixed together. Among the most widespread theoretical fictions that assume an expressive meaning for the cry, that of birth provides a rather clear schema of origin. The infant, *infans*, 'one who does not speak', enters the world with the inaugural cry of existence. Every cry from then on would refer back to this native and vital eruption. The non-verbal would belong to bare life, which motivates an association of the cry with animality, speechlessness, and the limited world of primal needs. The sounds uttered by animals are also always called cries, forgetting that there are animal sounds that humans do not hear, ultrasounds or infrasounds inaudible to our ears. In politics, the cry is associated, positively or negatively, with the plebs, in opposition to the sophisticated language of the elite. The cry of the people would be the voice of the voiceless that emerges without being articulable within the dominant order. The howl would derive from revolutionary insurrection. Still within a subversive register, the cry of madness adds to the prestige of the inarticulate voice: According to an old romantic idea, the madman is a bearer of truth — an idea that was reactivated for a time in the 1970s by the figure of the schizophrenic and through therapies designed to elicit the return of the primal scream and the externalization of buried psychic pain. Such is indeed the core of this expressive conception of the cry, based on the myth of interiority. The cry would be the vector of expulsion of what is inside, unknown, repressed. Its eruption as pure affect, archaic and monosemous, allows us to hear, in a state of bewilderment and so without analysis, an impulsive force of resistance to articulation. There even exist types of so-called radical music, like heavy metal, which use techniques of shouting or guttural voices, screaming at maximal intensity to saturate their sonic space. The fact, however, that this is a vocal "technique" should lead us to question the myth of the pure cry. Does not such utterance fall within some art, some construction of sound, unarticulated to be sure, but inscribed in codes?

The cry's voice

Hearing the cry within language implies moving beyond the simplistic opposition between the cry and the word, between the articulated and the unarticulated/inarticulate. In its manner of breathing and of intensifying the verbal flow, the cry operates within words and ideas. Artaud's brilliant intuition of meaning carried by breath before being bound by the syllable must undoubtedly be taken up with caution, which is to say without blindly giving all credit to the expressive function of the cry. His valuable critique of the notion of representation allowed him to conceive a new language for the stage. Criticizing representations that reiterate reality and betray it, Artaud puts in their place expression that stays as close as possible to the real. His thinking on the unarticulated/inarticulate nevertheless is not reducible to expressing some preverbal impulse or primal scream. Together with passions that cry out, like terror, joy, or pain, he mixed the artifices and timbres that compose a voice. The reevaluation of this preverbal, pre-syllabic foundation should not make us forget that, instead of original purity, there is always something composite, hybrid, figurative, and mediated in the breaths that lead to vocalization. Even Rousseau, whose history of language is founded on the expression of passions, underscored the role of figuration from the very first cries uttered by humans. In his *Essay on the Origin of Languages*, he wrote that "passions wrested the first voices,"[12] but he also noted that unarticulated sounds, like cries and groans, formed the first stages of voice and were refined in becoming verbal. The fact that cries, whether they are called first, natural, impulsive, etc., could have been mediated by or associated with other elements of communication allows us to hear what composes them beyond the pure affect they are thought to express. As a result, it is necessary to rediscover the work of sonic, material, and scriptural figuration that makes the cry something that is at once expressive and compositional: A cry is not limited to crying; it is not played out in the immediacy of its utterance — at least not for those artists, thinkers, and writers who let it out as a sound that drives their work.

It is therefore a challenge to preserve the power of the cry within articulated language and to make it heard from within words, sentences, and textual compositions. There are numerous ways to convey and release a cry in writing. Without doubt, Édouard Glissant's work is emblematic of such stakes, for it is entirely — whether in his poetry, novels, or philosophy — born from the intention to articulate the fundamental, original cry uttered by slaves in the hold of the slave ship. According to Glissant, who was of Martinican origin, this cry remains forever inaccessible to the extent that attempting to reproduce it directly and realistically would trivialize its tragic reality; such an attempt would be a betrayal. He makes it echo in the cry

12. Jean-Jacques Rousseau, *Essay on the Origin of Languages* (trans. John T. Scott; Dartmouth College, 1998), 293.

of the first slave who fled upon being disembarked in the West Indies to begin life in the wild. Faced with such tragedies, literature and historiography are confronted with the unrepresentable — a question endlessly discussed in the twentieth century and which continues to fuel debates on the representation of horror. Glissant's work does not directly seek this moment of the original cry, even if it is entirely inspired by it. It is made to take a *detour*. Lacking the ability to access this original cry and its excess beyond measure, we must invent measures other than representation and undertake a poetic work on language as a way of breathing the original and deafening cry. Glissant defines his writing in this way:

> What then is language? This cry that I elected? Not only the cry, but the *absence* beating in the cry. [...] And my language, rigid and dark or alive or strained is that lack first, then the will to slough the cry into speech before the sea.[13]

Words are thus inspired by the breath of such a cry, forever unrepresentable and requiring the artifice of poetic language to make itself heard. Accessing the memory of the cry thus demands losing any initial meaning and "set[ting] the word astray in the teeming deafness."[14] Poetic work on language supposes a disarticulation of prose as well as a rearticulation that invent a new regime of writing not indexed to representation but inspired at the sonic source of breaths and suffocations like the cry. This is what Artaud, in his own way, was trying to do on the stage, frustrating the formalism of representation and creating

13. Édouard Glissant, *Poetic Intention* (trans. Nathalie Stephens with Anne Malena; Nightboat Books, 2010), 37–38.
14. Édouard Glissant, *Sun of Consciousness* (trans. Nathanaël; Nightboat Books, 2020), 22.

word-gestures. For it is not enough to proclaim; one must also create conditions for listening, without which "we are quietly screaming. Our voices sink into the ground without echo. *The cry is an aborted root.*"[15]

The treatment of the cry in music undoubtedly demonstrates that it is never the pure and immediate expression of affect, contrary to the mythologies it provokes. Music allows us to hear the cry as articulable and not merely as a primal, impulsive, and uncontrolled belch. Nietzsche praised lyrical art by arguing that opera transforms the natural, ugly cry into an artificial cry that is sung and turned into an artistic sound. Certain cries are indeed integrated into musical scores. In the finale of Mozart's *Don Giovanni*, as the titular character descends into hell, it is less terror that emerges than the spectacular, auditory theater and dramatization of his scream. In a musical score, cries can be read among the notes and accompany indications of pitch, duration, and intensity. Tosca's *Ah!*, or that of her pursuers, in Puccini's opera, for example, are noted as "*alto grida*" or "*grida prolungate, lontane,*" and some notes must be sung "*gridando.*" The cry is vocalized and integrated into the sonic structure. Even in a work meant to be realistic, or veristic, like *Tosca*, an expressive cry, arising from tragic pain, is the result of convention, of sonic protocol, like the *hubris* of Greek tragedy, which transforms it into an artifact. It becomes a musical moment, one sound among others, even if not as precisely codified as a note. In the composer Luciano Berio's *Sequenza III*, modulations of the voice are associated with laughter, cries, moans, and whispers. This treatment disconnects the cry from the emotive source from which it supposedly derives. The cry becomes a vocal gesture freed from its expressive function:

15. Édouard Glissant, *A New Region of the World* (trans. Martin Munro; Liverpool University Press, 2023), 44.

Expression remains, but it no longer refers to a narrative or affective origin, but is placed in a series of sonic sequences, like an inexpressive expression. From an acoustic point of view, the cry can even blend into art music, sometimes without our being able to distinguish it from instrumental sounds.[16]

The cry can then be perceived as a facial expression, a manifestation of the body in air, a gesture-breath. It takes its meaning from a scale of aspects, in the sense that Wittgenstein uses this term, without necessarily expressing any particular emotion, like a face whose expressions seem to convey this or that feeling, but which is comprehensible and shareable only through habits and conventions.[17] Paired with a "scene" — theatrical or social — cries "express" fear, terror, or joy because they are inscribed into a network of affects and signs. The cry in itself, though non-linguistic, is in no way universal. While the ability to cry is human, the cry does not possess an expressive meaning independent of the scales of feelings or sonic values to which it is associated. This redefinition of the cry, made possible through its use in music, thus allows us to hear differently what is called a cry-text (*texte cri*) or an *éCRIture*. Listened to in the broader sonic substance that is breath, it is not essentially distinguishable from a whisper, which is not the opposite of a cry, but a modality of breath inscribed in the play of articulation and disarticulation proper to oral and written language. A murmur stretches speech toward silence. We must once again question the illusory generality of words like *cry* or *silence*, as though

16. See Maja Ratkje, *Concerto for Voice*.
17. See Ludwig Wittgenstein, *Culture and Value* (trans. Peter Winch; University of Chicago Press, 1980), 51.

they named *the* cry or *the* silence, for silence is less an absence of noise than a sonic device through which speech and writing resonate in their own, singular way.

V. Silences and Murmurs

Silence does not exist. Or at least it is a negation of noise. For a silence can stretch out, and such a paradox leads us to admit that silence is hearable in different ways even when there is total silence. *Listen to that silence!* Silence as the elimination of unwanted sounds becomes instead a sonic milieu that incites our ears to be newly attentive. Silence is sometimes described as deafening, so much does it alter our ordinary hearing and disrupt our perception. Rather curious experiences can be brought about by the deep silences of the countryside or of a library, by the absence of noise in an anechoic chamber, or by putting in earplugs. Adjectives or metaphors can be used to describe the color or aridity of different silences to distinguish them, for they do differ. Indeed in acoustics, silence doesn't depend on what the human ear can perceive, but on frequencies that are objectively detectable by measuring devices. Vibrations never cease; it is instead the listener's perceptual capacity that falters. Even when we are not aware of a silence's sonic qualities, they remain, to the point where sometimes we have to take them into account during recording. It is thus with ambient sounds that are part of a work, depending on whether they reverberate or absorb other sounds. When audio mixing, it might be necessary to record nothing, thereby recording the silence of a particular place to use later with recordings of voices or sounds made in the same place. As curious as it might seem, silence is recordable! In film or radio, an ambient slice serves to fill in gaps with such silence or to eliminate unwanted noises.

Listening to silences

The sound of silence is thus relative to a sonic environment where it plays several roles. In music, pauses and breaths do not interrupt the flow of a work, but join in the notes.

And even in the extreme case of a work of silence, like John Cage's *4'33"*, its performance at the piano implies the absence of sounds but implicates all of the noises surrounding the performance. Even more so, film, when it was "silent," was accompanied by music, and its images comprised sounds and voices that, even if one couldn't physically perceive them, resounded in the viewer's head, especially in expressionist films with their rather noisy faces. As Michel Chion suggested, such film was not silent, but deaf, which did not prevent it from being heard.[1] Proposing a subtle paradox, he wrote that the arrival of sound film allowed us at last to hear silence and to put on screen silent characters, like mute persons. It would thus be more fitting to say of a silent being, whether human or not, that they are being quiet. Silence, in the fullest sense, refers to that which is silent but can make noise or alter the soundspace. In this spirit, the Catalan composer Federico Mompou wrote a series of pieces for the piano titled *Música callada*, which means 'silent music' or 'quiet music'. Inspired by verses by John of the Cross, this piece is imbued with a powerful spirituality. A prayer attributed to John of the Cross incidentally reveals rather well this paradox of a silence that makes itself heard. He asks God to take him into his silence and to erase all worldly noises:

> Silence in me what is not of you, he implores, fill with your silence my being, which is too eager to speak, too inclined to noisy, outside action. Impose your silence even on my prayer so that it may be pure passion for You.

1. Michel Chion, *The Voice in Cinema* (trans. Claudia Gorbman; Columbia University Press, 1999), 95: "From the very outset there was an essential feature distinguishing the silent movies from canned pantomime. The silent film's characters were not mute, they spoke."

Nevertheless, the silence of this prayer, even in its interiority, is constituted by these words and voices, and it is first and foremost defined as the falling away of superfluous noises. The ideal of silence, whether as absolute nothingness or absolute presence, will never make the modalities of its sonic existence disappear.

In the same way that we have to free the cry from various discourses on the unarticulated or inarticulate, it is important to listen to silence in itself before projecting meaning onto it. Prayer, meditation, and concentration no doubt may require the absence of exterior noise. Still, silence does not necessarily predispose us to such activities. *Malentendus* related to silence come from its uses getting confused with its supposed nature. When linked to metaphysics, silence predisposes us to an awareness of the beyond, whether of death or of supersensible worlds. A minute of silence encourages us to think about the deceased, and the absence of noise is sometimes described as a "deathly silence." Unexplored extraterrestrial space is often described as silent, as though our lack of bearing or understanding imposed silence. The famous line by Pascal, "the eternal silence of these infinite spaces frightens me," encourages such mutism before the mystery of Creation. NASA's astrophysicists even had the idea in 1977 to pierce this interplanetary silence by sending forth earthly sounds — voices, cries, music, noises — on its *Voyager* probe. On the other hand, back on Earth, voluntary silence says more about political coercion than the call of the unknown. Whether censors condemn their opponents to silence or rebels forsake the linguistic regime of power, silence contains a message that makes it eloquent. Silence may be metaphysical or political, but it is always verbal and meaningful; silence "speaks"... doubtless a little too much, for its physical, acoustic presence disappears under the excess of meanings. Observing a silence while staying clear of interpretation means observing instead its anti-verbal effects and appreciating its densities and textures. Concretely, silence allows us to hear sound. Proust made this observation when he described the effect of earplugs. While, by blocking the ear canal, we make all those annoying noises — the street, the neighbors — progreswsively fade away, sometimes a louder sound pierces the earplug, and, suddenly, it all starts again:

> a shock, louder than the rest, manages to make itself heard, gentle as a sigh, unrelated to any other sound, mysterious; and the call for an explanation that it emits is sufficient to awaken us.[2]

2. Marcel Proust, *The Guermantes Way* (trans. C. K. Scott Moncrieff; Yale University Press, 2018), 77: "To return to the problem of sound, we have only to thicken the wads that plug the aural passages, and they confine to a pianissimo the girl who has just been playing a boisterous tune overhead; if we go further, and steep one of the wads in grease, at once the whole household must obey its despotic rule; its laws extend even beyond our portals. Pianissimo is not enough; the wad instantly closes the keyboard, and the music lesson is abruptly ended; the gentleman who was walking up and down in the room above breaks off in the middle of his beat; the movement of carriages and streetcars is interrupted as though a head of state were expected to pass. And indeed this attenuation of sounds sometimes disturbs our sleep instead of protecting it. Only yesterday the incessant noise in our ears, by describing to us in a continuous narrative all that was happening in the street and in the house, succeeded at length in making us sleep, like a boring book; today, on the surface of silence that is spread over our sleep a shock, louder than the rest, manages to make itself heard, gentle as a sigh, unrelated to any other sound, mysterious; and the call for an explanation that it emits is sufficient to awaken us. Take away for a moment from the sick man the cotton wool that has been plugging his ears and in a flash the daylight, the full sunlight of sound dawns afresh, dazzling him, is born again in the universe [...]."

Proust thus compares the listener's body to an instrument that can muffle or amplify a sound that strikes it. Silence opened his ears to sonic qualities that speech had covered over.

We listen to silence by being silent, by draining words of their power to name, by inundating the world and plugging up voids of meaning, however small. Silence derails language by its very existence and provokes a hemorrhaging of meanings. If it does not last, it may go unnoticed, but, should it continue unexpectedly, then comes discomfort, even panic. Nathalie Sarraute was brilliantly able to stage this devastating effect in a play with the very title *Silence*. We would have a hard time defining the subject of this play except to say that it deals with a moment of anxiety created by almost nothing: Speakers at a social gathering spar using intelligent and rather delicate remarks. One of the characters, however, remains silent, without explanation. Little by little, this silence brings about a disruption in the social codes, and each individual realizes the futility of their own pronouncements. Their reassuring babble no longer functions, and their social plenitude founders because of this mute presence. The hypertrophy of such a scene in which speakers seem to be in mortal danger underscores just how much silence can create a siphon through which linguistic regimes drain away. At the end of the play, a single word restores the speakers' sense of community. Less an absence than a method of evacuating, silence is active and sonic by contradiction. The paradox of writing silence comes from how it makes us hear the vanity of words, from how it decompresses them and brings them back to the breath of their origin.

Puncturing speech
Could a writer be defined as a propagator of silence in the middle of language? They would pierce the plenitude of meanings by breathing into it a dividing wind. Rather than making sentences sing, they would seek the resonance of what had been silenced by their excess of meaning. Pascal Quignard, recalling the long company he kept with silence and his taste for the residue of words, defines himself not as a spokesperson (*porte-parole*) but as a "silenceperson" (*porte-silence*). His path toward genuine listening is to stop speaking in order to hear anew the breath of language:

> To fall silent is first to tear oneself away from the deafness in which we exist with regard to the language within us and in which the speaker is entirely submerged in the social, rhythmic, ritual *circulus*.[3]

How is this first tacit moment, prior to speech, able to later maintain itself in the language of signs and images? A painting may be described as silent, Quignard suggests in reference to the paintings of Georges de la Tour. As was the case for the cry, the question of the representation of silence leads us to rethink what it is meant to express.

Cries and silence — both are related to the unarticulated breath, to the point that a silence might be cried and a cry might be silent. In his seminar on 17 March 1965, Jacques Lacan analyzed Munch's famous painting, *The Scream* (*Le Cri*, in French), in this way, choosing it to propose a reversal: Observing that the character represented in the act of screaming with their mouth open also has their hands on their ears, Lacan suggested that the cry imposes silence. In place of the obvious account in which a cry is uttered against a background of silence, which it pierces,

3. Pascal Quignard, *The Hatred of Music* (trans. Matthew Amos and Fredrik Rönnbäck; Yale University Press, 2016), 87.

Lacan affirms instead that the cry *provokes* silence, playing on this verb, *provoke*, which signifies the call of a voice. He pursues his commentary with reference to Wilhelm Fliess, Freud's friend, underscoring that silence remains tightly linked to verbalization: It is less that silence indicates a withdrawal or defense than that it shows the presence of drives, unobjectivizable and inarticulable, at the heart of speech.[4] From this impossibility, Lacan will go on to develop his analysis of the voice as a part-object (*objet partiel*) of desire, which can be articulated by fetishizing it. Still, what interests us here concerns listening to silence insofar as it is housed in speech. And this silence — which listeners are quick to want to fill for it is unbearable — can significantly modify the function of language. In discussing language and their use of it, many philosophers have sought to plug up any voids through which their meaning might evacuate uncontrollably. During the dinners he organized, Kant dreaded moments of silence, and he constructed tricks to continually restart conversation. Even if it meant talking about subjects of no great importance, like the weather, he thought up artificial transitions and dubious analogies to reduce any silences to mere pauses in conversation.[5]

Lacan, on the contrary, used — indeed abused — silence in his seminars, sometimes interrupting his delivery for half a minute in the middle of a demonstration. Claude Jaeglé studied these "voids at the heart of the psychoanalyst's theory" and suggests that they participate in an experience of living thought:

4. Jacques Lacan, *Séminaire XII*, http://staferla.free.fr/S12/S12%20PROBLEMES.pdf

5. Immanuel Kant, *Anthropology from a Pragmatic Point of View* (trans. Victor Lyle Dowdell; Southern Illinois University Press, 1996), 190.

> He utters an idea aloud and tries to hear what the utterance of this idea allows us to hear in this affect of intensified resonance engendered by the presence of an audience.[6]

Jaeglé also observes the phenomena of breath that accompany both speech and silence: bellows, sighs, and roars, which play with unarticulated sounds. These moments make us hear a continuum of echoes between orator and audience, at the risk of stretching out the resonance of ideas along a vertiginous spectrum. Whatever judgments we might make about this type of theoretical performance, we can see in it an original conceptualization and use of silence at odds with the obsessive tendency philosophers have to fill silences with extra meaning.

Listening to silence through its effects at the heart of speech, and more generally at the heart of language, thus contributes to our recognition of the sonic part of thought, both oral and written. If silence can haunt an orator's voice, this is because silence maintains the presence of something unarticulated in it, a breath that constitutes the driving force of expression. We then may hear meanings that are otherwise immediately made covert by our mastery of semantics and grammar, so long as they float to our listening ears and circulate in discrete resonances. A wandering, undisciplined, inattentive listening sometimes produces unexpected effects, allowing us to pierce the flow of words and seize in little silences a tone, a breath, a grunt that reveals a meaning or the speaker's disposition to the world.

6. Claude Jaeglé, *Portrait silencieux de Jacques Lacan* (Presses Universitaires de France, 2010), 25. Chantal Thomas also highlights the important role of silence and suspension in Roland Barthes's seminars: "Scandalous in a place of public speech (and teaching), silence played a significant role there. Rather than emphasizing the impact and pertinence of his message, emphasis was instead diverted toward speech that was suspended and trying to find itself, toward something unsaid, a void." *Pour Roland Barthes* (Seuil, 2015), 29.

To describe this disposition, we should, moreover, propose some other expression than "worldview" — that calque of the German *Weltanschauung*, which gets so over used in philosophy. A worldhearing, a different "way of listening," would be an alternative to such visual objectification. This hearing is manifest in the driving breath of intelligence, which, even in its silent form, can also be heard in writing. As Marguerite Duras declared: "Writing also means not speaking. Keeping silent. Screaming without sound."[7] Indeed the cries uttered in her work, both literary and cinematic, like those of the Vice-Consul of Lahore in her novel/play/film *India Song*, can be heard just as Lacan suggested: sounds where silence rushes in.

Writing silence, or rather listening to silence in writing, puts language and its sonic dimension into question precisely at the moment sound disappears from it. For then, sounds engorged with meanings give way to other sounds, rustlings that are part of the breath and carry other meanings. Gaston Bachelard described this "basic economy of breath" that makes a human being "a 'sound chamber.'"[8] Prior to sentences spoken, the desire to speak first manifests as an effort to breathe and produce sounds. A good reader — one with their ears open — hears beneath words this elementary breath that carries meaning. Bachelard observed that even when reading "silently" a reader cannot help but mime a pneumatic movement he called "silent speech."[9] Such silence carries meaning and differs from a willful, denying silence, for rather than blocking off breath, it deploys it in language.

7. Marguerite Duras, *Writing* (trans. Mark Polizzotti; University of Minnesota Press, 2011), 17.
8. Gaston Bachelard, *Air and Dreams* (trans. Edith R. Farrell and C. Frederick Farrell; The Dallas Institute, 1988), 239–40.
9. *Ibid.*, ch. 12.

Shhh!

Some writers have taken up this inverse inspiration that contests the delicate music of style and sometimes makes writing fail. For this reason, the way they work with the material of language — sign, sound, and sense —provides a good number of insights into the presence of sound in thoughts, images, and words. Samuel Beckett is doubtless the person who took this work of silence at the heart of speech the furthest, to its most extreme auditory outcomes. His career as a creator allows us to hear most closely what words, and even voices, are like when they return to minimal breath, to the slightest murmur. Unlike literary history, which highlights only a few of Beckett's masterpieces and downplays the textual, filmic, and theatrical works from the end of his creative life, we can assert, on the contrary, that these so-called experimental works on the image and minimal sound are the culmination of his entire oeuvre.

Beckett practiced the inversion of language to the advantage of sonic matter through sometimes infinitesimal gestures, for example in the use of silent film. A brief moment of his cinematographic work, *Film*, demonstrates the paradox of an injunction to silence. In 1964, Beckett drafted a film script and accompanied its director, Alan Schneider, to New York. He chose the anachronistic style of silent film and had a once-famous actor, Buster Keaton, hired to play the lead. Beckett insisted on an extremely rigorous visual protocol and also demanded that one sound, but only one, be heard in this twenty-minutes film: "Shhh," which is whispered by a female character requesting silence with her finger on her lips. This sole sound erupts to silence us, and the hearing viewer thus hears a call to not make noise and to open their ears to listen to something despite watching a silent film. In this oddity is revealed the process Beckett would pursue to the last limits of the audible, which he called the *least* (*moindre*). Indeed, he tirelessly sought to reduce visual and sonic elements, notably voices, in order to divert them from their expressive function and to treat them as minimal elements, available for new perceptions.

From the start of his literary career, Beckett never ceased to impose silence on language by exhausting the desire to speak, to talk about "subjects," or to construct castles out of words.[10] The war he waged on style aimed to break the expressivity of words and sentences meant to convey ideas and feelings. It has often been said that Beckett made language stutter, whether it was English or French, and that he did so bringing the "old style" to its end, finishing it off. But this project also sought to mobilize another function of language. In the same year as *Film*, he wrote a radio play titled *Words and Music*, which staged a row between a voice embodying "words" and an orchestra seeking to express them. Any expressive link between the two is constantly mocked. By dissociating speech and music, Beckett makes us hear the expressive inexpressiveness of both. Playing with the artificial link between a particular melody or violin piece and a particular feeling, he empties these expressive effects of their meaning. In several television plays as well, he reinterpreted certain "expressive" musical works along this anti-expressive scheme. He did so with *Ghost Trio*, where the measures of the second movement of Beethoven's "Ghost" Trio (op. 70 no. 1), *Largo assai ed espressivo*, are articulated with camera movements that follow a progressive lowering of the volume. So too again with *Nacht und Träume*, where the last seven measures of Schubert's lied are hummed in a low voice until that voice goes out.

10. Beckett insisted that his directors respect the duration of his plays' silences.

The erasure of a speaking or singing voice raises questions about what speaking wishes to say or to silence. When language stutters to the point of exhausting speech, it delivers the minimum sound of its meanings in the form of echoes. The vocal system gives way to a mouth that speaks on its own. Thinking subjects become air ducts through which dead or fragmented voices pass. Speaking bodies have their mode of presence changed, becoming increasingly breathy: At the end of exhaustion and diminishment, there is not emptiness, but a back-and-forth of inhalations and exhalations. For *breath* is not reducible to a stream of air, but manifests the movement of a body in its minimal reality. Beckett's work on sound transforms his characters into sonic corporealities that fade away without ever going out completely. Deleuze knew how to describe this energy, defining Beckett's television plays as "breath-images" that do not last long but concentrate intensities.[11] Beckett's 1969 *Breath* presents this minimal phenomenon in twenty seconds: Starting from darkness, a faint cry is heard, followed by an inhalation accompanied by an increase in light, then an exhalation that ends with the same faint cry. Silence and cry combine within a composition of breaths. Does the performance boil down to some purified form? It doubtless suggests more, for listening to these whispers and breaths in Beckett's final pieces abolishes all psychological depth in favor of a persistent resonance. It makes us hear the voice beneath the words, the murmur beneath the voice, and then the sonic residues that continue the breath of the voices that have come undone. The work of disarticulation that many writers

11. Gilles Deleuze, "The Exhausted" (trans. Anthony Uhlmann), *Substance* 78:3–28, 19.

have undertaken on language, through cries and silence, aspires no less than to relearn how to listen to voices and to the multiplicity of sonic phenomena that compose them.

VI. The Notion of Soundscape and its Ambiguities

The voice, when returned to the notion of breath, reemerges in the domain of sounds, freed of its expressive function and rid of mythologies of inspiration. It loses its unicity and its uniqueness of timbre, composed instead of a diversity of components. After such a decomposition, it's useful to come back with new ears to the sonic components that vibrate in a thought or a piece of writing. The musical model should be abandoned in favor of a less sacred acoustic approach that would no longer seek melodies or harmonies in sentences but instead embrace noise. Thought can thus be heard more than as a vector for the voice, but as a sonic milieu. Such a conversion is only possible thanks to technological and aesthetic revolutions that have occurred in the history of listening, in particular since the Industrial Revolution. Even if the nineteenth and twentieth centuries do not hold a monopoly on attending to sounds, our ordinary, aesthetic perception has seen a disruption to sonic hierarchies distinguishing good sounds from bad. City sounds might not necessarily have changed in intensity from the past but they have changed in kind. Historiographical studies have begun to show what kinds of sounds city or country dwellers could have heard, as well as in what ways and according to what values they heard them.[1] Noise was relegated to the sphere of the masses, the peasantry, or animals, clearly marking a division between sonic worlds according to social rank.

Acoustic revolutions

Nevertheless, the irruption of industrial sounds in the nineteenth century and the reconfiguration of acoustic spaces linked to modern urbanism radically modified ways of hearing. We can perceive how this sonic environment

1. See in particular the work of Arlette Farge on the noises of the street in *Essai pour une histoire des voix au XVIIIe siècle* (Bayard, 2009).

altered the collective psyche and the way the world was listened to in the texts of writers who were either terrified by or receptive to these modernities. Walter Benjamin thus highlighted how Baudelaire embodied the new *flâneur*, one who immerses themselves in the city and its crowds as if in a concert of noise.[2] While historians have studied the influence of the new public lighting on representations of nighttime, it is important to consider as well changes to acoustic spaces. Transformations in urban planning, especially in Paris during the time of Napoleon III and Haussmann's renovations, not only affected traffic and views, but also changed ways of hearing, supporting new types of noise and their modes of vibration. George Sand described the sense of security provided by the *grands boulevards*, compared to the small, murderous streets of old, and her description signals a change in auditory attention: Instead of keeping an ear out for suspicious noises, she allows herself to indulge in reverie.[3] These same grand avenues caused a dissociation of acoustic spaces, between those of public and private life. The urban flow made street peddlers' words less distinct, in favor of full and continuous noise. Meanwhile, bourgeois residences became ever more sealed off to escape this elevated noise level. Urban modernity must thus be analyzed in tune with such auditory transformations: Populations do not hear the same noises from one age to the next, but above all, they do not listen in the same way.

Any transformation of acoustics or hearing goes beyond a matter of physics or technology; it disrupts ways of thinking, writing, composing, and representing. Intellectual and

2. See Walter Benjamin, *Paris capitale du XIXe siècle : Le Livre des passages* (Cerf, 1997) and Aimée Boutin, *City of Noise: Sound and Nineteenth-Century Paris* (University of Illinois Press, 2015).
3. See George Sand, "La rêverie à Paris" (in *Paris Guide par les principaux écrivains et artistes de la France*; La Découverte, 1983).

artistic revolutions are indeed tightly linked to the modernization of cities, whether Barcelona, Paris, Vienna, or New York, where the avant-gardes were most active.[4] New noises emerged little by little in nineteenth-century literature to become materials for creation. This auditory change manifested itself in three ways: first in the increased interest of writers, philosophers, and artists in sound in their works; then in their work with sounds, especially those sounds that would have once been relegated to the chaos of noise; and finally in their acoustic approach to works as soundscapes. On an initial, referential level, engines, like that of the train, irrupted into realist descriptions.
The train, which also left its mark at the origin of film, attracted the attention of readers' ears, as in Émile Zola's *La bête humaine* (1890), a novel that mentions locomotive sounds prolifically, whether whistles blowing, brakes screeching, or strident, rhythmic chugging. In 1923, the composer Arthur Honegger transcribed the train's orchestral sounds in *Pacific 231*. Engine noises — trains, cars, or airplanes — invaded literature to the point that one writer, Edith Wharton, could write *A Motor-Flight Through France* in 1908 to narrate her car trips in which she was sometimes accompanied by Henry James, who was also an enthusiast of motorized adventures. As Proust wrote: "in all haste the horde of exiled sounds returns."[5]

Real sonic transformation occurs when sound abandons its role as realist reference to become the primary material of creation. This required the aesthetic revolution of transcending the hierarchy of harmonious sounds and noise, discovering the beauty of industrial sounds, treating them

4. I analyzed these disruptions in *Avant-Gardes et Modernité* (Hachette, 2000).
5. Marcel Proust, *The Guermantes Way* (trans. C. K. Scott Moncrieff; Yale University Press, 2018), 77. Translation modified.

as material, dehumanizing them, and making them the principal vectors of linguistic and pictorial creation. For the Futurists of the beginning of the twentieth century, sound was no longer a motif; it became a subject in itself and was brought to the foreground. As F. T. Marinetti asserted in his manifesto:

> A racing car with a hood that glistens with large pipes resembling a serpent with explosive breath ... a roaring automobile that seems to ride on grapeshot — that is more beautiful than the *Victory of Samothrace*.[6]

A vocabulary of sounds enlivens such enthusiastic writings about the engines of locomotives, ocean liners, and airplanes, "whose propeller flaps at the wind like a flag and seems to applaud like a delirious crowd."[7] At the same moment, Guillaume Apollinaire evoked the modern noises of the city thus: "The tramways, green fires on their backs, set their mechanical madness to music as far as the rails reach."[8]

The preeminence of sound, or at least its presence as a central stake of artistic creation, is as evident in poetry as it is in theater and, naturally, music. Protocols of enunciation and vocal practices get transformed. This is the case with Marinetti's instructions in his 1916 *Dynamic and Synoptic Declamation* for dehumanizing speech:

6. F. T. Marinetti, *The Founding and Manifesto of Futurism* (in *Futurism, an Anthology*, eds. Lawrence Rainey, Christine Poggi, and Laura Wittman; Yale University Press, 2009), 51.
7. *Ibid.*, 52.
8. Guillaume Apollinaire, "La chanson du Mal-Aimé" (in *The Penguin Book of French Verse: The Twentieth Century*, trans. Anthony Hartley; Penguin, 1959).

> Therefore the Futurist declaimer must [...] metallize, liquefy, vegetalize, petrify, and electrify his voice, merging it with the vibrations of matter itself as expressed by words-in-freedom.[9]

Along these lines, the composer Luigi Russolo wrote a foundational text for a new way of listening: *The Art of Noises*. This manifesto from 1913, which Russolo would later openly both claim and deny credit for, established a number of principles that revolutionized the status of sounds in music, and in the arts more generally, for the twentieth century. In this anti-musical approach, one is to embrace noise in order to discover other aesthetic objects at a remove from the established harmonies and tones to which we have become accustomed by musical instruments. Russolo demands that "we [...] break out of this restricted circle of pure sounds and conquer the infinite variety of noise-sounds."[10] He thus wished to take in the noises of streetcars, the shouts of the crowd, animal cries, the diverse breaths of nature, etc., to orchestrate them in a modern score. Recognizing the aesthetics of "impure" sounds opens the way to new thoughts and works in a sonic world that has clusters, which is to say amalgams of sounds that we are used to ignoring or rejecting as the brouhaha of the street. More generally, Russolo's manifesto is an invitation to a listening that is inclusive of all sonic phenomena, wheresoever they come from, without hierarchy, and as infinitely combinatorial.

9. F. T. Marinetti, *Dynamic and Synoptic Declamation* (in *Futurism, an Anthology*, eds. Lawrence Rainey, Christine Poggi, and Laura Wittman; Yale University Press, 2009), 221.
10. Luigi Russolo, *The Art of Noises: A Futurist Manifesto* (in *Futurism, an Anthology*, eds. Lawrence Rainey, Christine Poggi, and Laura Wittman; Yale University Press, 2009), 134.

The history of art music in the twentieth century becomes closely linked to this introduction of noise-sounds starting in the 1920s by composers like Edgard Varèse, who put the sound of sirens into his works *Amériques* in 1921 and *Ionisation* in 1929. The use of electricity and electroacoustic advances fed this transformation in listening, notably in the 1940s with *musique concrète* ('concrete music') and the studies of Pierre Schaeffer, who proposed "sound objects" (*objets sonores*) and acousmatic objects, which is to say objects no longer tied to their source of emission. A new typology of sounds followed from this, as well as a different art of hearing, which Schaeffer analyzed into four dispositions: *écouter* ('to listen'), taking a sound as an indicator of a source; *ouïr* ('to perceive (aurally)'), passively receiving a sensed sound; *entendre* ('to hear'), selecting a sound; *comprendre* ('to comprehend'), assigning meaning and value to the sound.[11] While these reflections might seem to be limited to the domain of musical creation, they go far beyond it, both because they are inspired by transformations in acoustic culture and because they participate in new conceptions and new practices of sound. This is why a true archaeology of listening must take into account modern technologies just as much as it does contemporary conceptual discourses and artistic activities. In this way, computer sound processing contributed to the conceptualization of sound as material and to furthering movements like *musique spectrale* ('spectral music'), and it continues to transform our understanding of sounds and voices. Unfortunately, professional philosophers have remained rather deaf both to technical issues, such as those of musical informatics, and to works of contemporary

11. Michel Chion, *Guide des objets sonores : Pierre Schaeffer et la recherche musicale* (Buchet-Chastel, 1983), 25.

music.[12] The treatment of the voice by Karlheinz Stockhausen in *Stimmung* or by Berio in *Sequenza III*, however, says much more about the relation of voice to subjectivity, meaning, duration, and listening than do many discussions in the humanities on the meaning of speech.

The way sounds are listened to, especially those that make up a voice, depends closely on the acoustic culture of the times. As a result, modes of thinking and writing too are contingent on the sonic environments in which they are forged. The history of literature and philosophy shows rare but fruitful exchanges between writing, thought, and music, such as those between Adorno and Schönberg, Jankélévitch and French music, or Toni Morrison and jazz. And yet, we must seek the presence of the sonic less in inspiration, in commentary, or in some analogy between sonic structures and written forms, than in changes to the ear. A revolution in sound, clearly perceptible in the twentieth century, manifests itself in those arts that contributed to the incorporation of new noises and to the reevaluation of sonic hierarchies. This revolution also came about in the sonic ecology of societies and especially in modes of listening, transforming the way sound enters our ears and how we perceive its arrangements. Emerging from such a cultural shift, the concept of "soundscape" marks a change in perspective.

Sonic ecologies

For noises to form a landscape, it is not necessary for them to be integrated into some musical score. In themselves and along the spectrum of listening, they can be heard as if they were connected, even if no prior artistic intention established such a link. As early as the late 1960s, the Canadian

12. The meeting of Boulez, Foucault, Deleuze, and Barthes at IRCAM in 1978, though famous, remained unproductive.

composer, R. Murray Schafer, proposed the term *soundscape* to signify this kind of listening, and this coinage has been rather successful across different disciplinary fields, especially thanks to the publication of his work *The Tuning of the World*. The translation of *soundscape* into French as *paysage sonore* ('sonic landscape') poses several problems due to the inappropriate analogy between the visual and the sonic, as the notion of landscape is heir to a long-standing literature on the gaze.[13] To be sure, the word *soundscape* remains close to *landscape*; however, the sonic must be heard in a language other than that of the visual. Despite this difficulty in translation, or thanks to it, the landscape dimension of a set of sounds introduces a small revolution in the way we listen to unintentional noises. Freed from an aesthetic judgment that decides what is harmonious or beautiful, this listening is a circumstantial cut in the sonic environment. It does not claim universality, but depends on both context and revocable conventions, allowing us to appreciate a composition of sounds as if it constituted a coherent landscape — *as if* implying that there is not, a priori, a framework delimiting which sounds go together. This falls under a Baudelairean approach,

13. R. Murray Schafer considered these problems of language thus: "It was very difficult to find a translation. The first time I came to Paris, we looked for a fitting term, and there were different proposals, as, for example, *relief sonore* ('sonic relief'). Then someone found the expression *paysage sonore* ('sonic landscape'). That worked, and we did the same for other languages, like German. Nevertheless, the choice of words is very important, and the expression *paysage sonore* differs from the word *soundscape*. The neutral character of term *soundscape* disappears when it is put in direct relation to the notion *landscape*. When I was in Poland, someone wanted to translate it with *sonosphère* ('soundsphere'), which would have better expressed this requirement of neutrality. But, oh well, today the expression *paysage sonore* has been accepted, and the important thing is to know what it is." Quoted in Carlotta Darò, "Architectes du son. Entretiens avec Pierre Mariétan et R. Murray Schafer," *Sonorités* 3 (December 2008),145–56.

open to the modernity of new forms of beauty that are changing and unexpected. The poet who wrote *The Spleen of Paris* knew well how to integrate urban phenomena into a landscape spectrum that previously lacked them, whether movements of the crowd, the crash of the glass-vendor's cargo, the correspondences of hearing to other senses, etc. It is up to the poetic gaze to select a visual or sonic landscape, like a group of clouds passing in the sky, or like the rubbing of fabric in an otherwise deafening street. For the grouping of disparate elements to become a quasi-artistic compound, both randomness and selection are necessary. A landscape is constituted according to criteria that are at once subjective, linked to a particular ear, and objective, stemming from a culture that values certain noises. Against a backdrop of passivity that leads us to receive heterogeneous noises, our listening can decide to select them in order to put them together. Inspired by the writings of Murray Schafer, the musician Bernie Krause thus left electronic music behind in the 1970s to instead record the sounds of nature, becoming a "bioacoustician." Equipped with headphones and recording devices that allowed him to make selections from a sonic environment, he captured the noises of animals and of the forest over thousands of hours of recordings. This immersive, selective listening produced recordings that, in their own right, rival sonic works of art, to the point that Krause called a work he believed captured the music that was already there in nature *The Great Animal Orchestra: Symphony for Orchestra and Wild Soundscapes* (2014).

The notion of *soundscape* is closely linked to an ecological and, more generally, political conception of sound: It does not invent a way of listening, but rather underscores that any listening, through its modes of attention, is inscribed in a political relation to sonic habitats.

One of Krause's objectives has been to make us hear the disappearance of any number of animal sounds, which is to say the disappearance of any number of species due to our current human-made ecological disaster. Schafer, with similar intention, denounced noise pollution, which erases certain "landscapes," and his recordings aim at preserving the memory of environments where a harmony reigned between "natural" and "human" sounds, all the while refuting any such distinction separating humans from nature. This is the case for soundscapes where sounds of the ocean, of animals, and of boats mingle, but which are disappearing due to industrialization and urbanization. Schafer believed that "the general acoustic environment of a society can be read as an indicator of social conditions which produce it and may tell us much about the trending and evolution of that society."[14] Being able to notice soundscapes thus leads us to become aware of the state of a society and how it functions. The ear thereby acquires a heuristic virtue, which is to say, an intellectual acuity for analyzing and understanding the surrounding world along a vector other than sight: a vector of listening, not a point of view. The World Soundscape Project was an educational program in the 1970s for listening to sonic environments, conceived with the critical intention of targeting industrial noise pollution and promoting an ecology of acoustic environments. Such an approach radically changes the relation of human subjects to sound. Rather than being passive faced with sonic material that insidiously infiltrates our bodies, we humans can actively change the sonic environment in which we are immersed in order to constrict it, compose it, and thus become conscious agents of these acoustic phenomena. From alienated listeners, we become

14. R. Murray Schafer, *The Soundscape: Our Sonic Environment and the Tuning of the World* (Destiny Books, 1994), 7.

composers of our environment. The ultimate question for a sonic ecology, Schafer specifies, is posed thus: "Is the soundscape of the world an indeterminate composition over which we have no control, or are we its composers and performers, responsible for giving it form and beauty?"[15] This is no less than an anthropological metamorphosis founded on an active listening to the world.
As Brandon LaBelle has written in a more explicitly political manner: "To enact one's freedom of listening is to necessarily aim for a broader and richer engagement with the range of voices to be heard and shared."[16]

Sonic ecology, like all schools of thought that use the word *ecology*, rests on a philosophy of nature and its habitation. Doubtless, one would have to distinguish among different worldviews, or rather different world-listenings, whose presuppositions are debatable and, indeed, debated. In the theories just presented, the philosophical presence of Henry David Thoreau is palpable. His book, *Walden; or, Life in the Woods*, has provided a model for conceiving what a beautiful soundscape is. It takes up the edenic presupposition of a simple life thought to preserve an original harmony, and it pursues the mythology present in Western literature and philosophy that pits such a life against the artifice of urban civilization, with its inequalities and discords. Indeed, in *Walden*, when recounting his life in an isolated cabin in Massachusetts, Thoreau notes precise sounds and their vibrations among the noises of the trees, which he compares to musical instruments, as if nature were an orchestra sending forth melodies for those who whished to hear them. The idea of a nature, or even a cosmos, arranged according to natural or supernatural

15. *Ibid.*, 5.
16. Brandon LaBelle, *Sonic Agency: Sound and Emergent Forms of Resistance* (Goldsmiths Press, 2018), 160.

harmonies goes back to ancient Greece and to the famous Pythagorean theory of a "music of the spheres." It stems from an analogy between world and music, and it underlies a poetic approach to soundscapes. Schafer's book, *The Tuning of the World*, even if it has been much debated theoretically, has a poetic charm, though outdated, that enchants the description of natural environments and their noises. The wind gets associated with the sounds of birds, insects, and fish; the waves of the sea resemble voices that the author relates to a maternal womb .... Nevertheless, this recourse to a poetic imaginary of nature does not prevent us from questioning the implicit categories on which such a discourse opposing countryside to city is based. The notion of "natural sound" indeed poses theoretical problems, for a sound coming from a forest is not necessarily more natural than the sound of an engine, unless we fall back on the metaphysical antithesis of nature and culture, of animality and humanity. By qualifying city noises as pollutants, singers of the soundscape reinstate old aesthetic values that deny urban life the capacity to reinvent beauty. An ideology of decline or decadence is not far off, which would denounce the inanity of new worlds to go instead in search of lost landscapes. I analyze below the political stakes of such a listening to sounds we call *natural* in opposition to those invasive noises of the city with its electric and amplified sounds.

Despite its underlying and debatable aesthetic judgments, highlighting soundscapes has straightaway the merit of sociologically sketching out acoustic communities. Sounds indeed offer landmarks by which we can characterize sonic environments, styles, or "familial airs," which is to say their family resemblances (*airs de famille*), though *airs* is even more apt for sound as the word *air* refers to both breath and music. These resemblances as airs can, through rigorous analysis, be described with a precise lexicon. It is not enough to distinguish categories of noise based on their sources — a truck engine and an electric saw in one group, the song of a bird and the rustling of leaves in another. The volumes, pitches, and onsets of sounds, their differentials and their durations — all of these constitute markers of soundscapes. Schafer's proposals are numerous, and instead of founding a method and giving its principles and tools, he shows that many modes of listening are possible, like family resemblances: not essences, but groups according to a chosen classificatory criterion with different sonographic schema. Among these, he emphasizes the degree of fidelity sounds have to their source, depending on whether the listener can identify their distinct origins or hears instead an indistinct brouhaha. Engine noises in the city generally produce sounds of low fidelity, while quieter spaces allow precise, high-fidelity sounds to emerge. Habitats, identified according to precise criteria, are characterized by soundscapes that correspond to technical advances and, equally, to social evolutions, like whether there is television, whether a beltway or other road is nearby, or the level of voices around a table. To analytical ears, these are cultural markers, and, increasingly, sociologists, anthropologists, and historians are taking them into account. The notion of soundscape has indeed oriented our listening toward issues with stakes that are as aesthetic as they are political. It can also allow us to hear the sound of texts more precisely, the sound of the soundscapes they describe, as well as the sound of the rhythms and breaths at work in writing.

The analysis of soundscapes can be quite rewarding when reading texts, whether literary, of course, but also philosophical or historical, so long as we pay attention to them. To read with our ears is to be aware of soundscapes in at least two ways. First, we hear sounds that are familiar to us and that we easily identify as soundscapes. We are particularly sensitive to those environments we belong to, with their different facets and associations. We hear them because our attention was formed through an education that had us pick out sounds and put them into a hierarchy, neglecting some in order to be captivated by others. Our culture leads us to enjoy soundscapes where ugly sounds are unbearable — ugly sounds being those that are inappropriate, strange, or interruptive, like a klaxon during a Brahms quartet. Our ears remain shaped by rules for associating sounds that come to form familial airs. Our ears are bound to convention and history, changing with changes in world view and sound technologies. This is the case with some of the mountain noises, songs and waterfalls, that appear in the soundscapes praised by Romantic writers, and even by authors like Rousseau or Senancour before them. Literature, of course, did not need to wait for these writers to bring forth the sound of a stream, but with them, such a sound brings together new sonic ensembles and creates harmonies of words, signs, and sounds. Inversely, as we noted above, the enthusiastic embrace of industrial, urban modernity by the avant-gardes of the early twentieth century gave rise to new modes of listening and new soundscapes. Sonic family resemblances change within a single community and reconfigure its sensibilities, its modes of attention, and its social and aesthetic hierarchies of value.

What's more, listening to the soundscapes of a piece of writing offers us an approach more subtle than the sociological tagging of acoustic environments. It notices the presence of sonic elements in writing itself, in its inspiration and exhalation, as we suggested regarding cries and whispers. It is thus less about identifying a familial air in an acoustic community than it is about identifying the singularities of an author who allows us, consciously or not, to hear the composition of rhythms and breaths regulating their relation to words and writing. So it is for Proust as read by Walter Benjamin who, with a certain audacity, detected in both Proust's correspondence and *In Search of Lost Time* the sickly breath of an asthmatic:

> This asthma became part of his art — if indeed his art did not create it. Proust's syntax rhythmically and step by step reproduces his fear of suffocating. And his ironic, philosophical, didactic reflections invariably are the deep breath with which he shakes off the weight of memories. On a larger scale, however, the threatening, suffocating crisis was death, which he was constantly aware of, most of all while he was writing.[17]

To be sure, Benjamin's reading, despite its grand ambition for a physiology of style, is questionable insofar as a reader, rather than feeling suffocated, could be sensitive to the immense respiration of Proustian sentences, which are periodic and greatly extended. Nevertheless, he orients our attention to the question of sound in the very movement of writing and thinking, linking respiration to psychological phenomena, like anxiety, and to the very syntax of writing. This Benjaminian intuition is all the more legitimate since Proust did indeed show extreme care with his sonic environment. His desire to isolate himself from surrounding noises, like those of the street, by means of the cork-lined walls of his apartment brings about a peculiar acoustics for writing. The smallest noise, like a bath being run downstairs or a pen on paper, became pronounced. Although the sonic environment in which an author writes is not the same for the writing itself, and although we would need to

17. Walter Benjamin, "The Image of Proust" (in *Illuminations*, trans. Harry Zohn; Schocken, 1968), 214.

distinguish the physical observation of working conditions from syntactic analysis, the acoustic means of creation and the relation of the writing subject to this environment are assuredly involved in the making of ideas and sentences. We shall see more precisely how writing is a matter of sound mixing. For now, let us observe the importance of the sonic environment for the composition and transformation of language and thought. Disruptions brought about by acoustic devices, like the telephone, radio, or tape recorder, offer striking examples.

VII. Acoustic Modernities and Thought Experiments

Do bodies breathe and hear differently depending on the era and society in which they live? Breathing is such a universal given that listening to the breaths and rhythms present in a piece of writing or the elaboration of a thought applies to texts from different times and cultures. Nevertheless, a warning from anthropology leads us to observe unique ways of breathing, even if only in terms of language, as each language involves particular bodily arrangements. Even within a single culture, the model for breathing too has a history based on the evolution of means of communication and acoustic devices. Individuals are obviously influenced by the conditions under which they express themselves for how they project their voice, evaluate its reception, and insert it into a sonic environment. These changes appear even more markedly when new devices alter how we listen and speak. Above we noted with Benjamin the influence asthma had on Proust's writing, but it seems even safer to inquire into the acoustic devices that appeared during his lifetime and the interest they aroused in him.

The telephonic voice

Approaching the sonic environment of an individual, both the sounds they heard and those they emitted, requires being attentive to acoustics and sound equipment. Regarding Proust, much has been said about *In Search of Lost Time*'s Vinteuil Sonata that accompanies Swann's inner emotions, although we have not been able to definitively identify the composer who might have inspired it. Nevertheless, it is also instructive to study the relation between interior and exterior sounds that the writer constructed by subscribing, in 1911, to the *théâtrophone*, which was a telephone system connected to opera houses that allowed people to listen to performances from their homes. It was thus that Proust, alone in his soundproofed apartment, brought the operas of Wagner and Debussy into his ears according to an acoustic rather different from the public and immersive acoustics of a concert hall. Some commentators have detected in this an intensity of listening that is indicative of the attention to sound in *In Search of Lost Time*.[1] More generally, Proust thereby discovered an "acousmatic" device, which is to say a device that dissociates the perception of sounds from the sight of their source. Music and sounds reach the ear without the listener being able to visualize the site of their emission, save through the imagination. They exist by themselves, in the audition of them, and they achieve an autonomy suitable for composing soundscapes and for becoming associated with other sensory phenomena. Acousmatic sounds, like those propagated by the telephone, float in perceptive consciousness and can be listened to without the musical instruments that emit them or the voices that utter them. The importance of this new relation to the sonic environment induced by the modern use of the telephone is evident in a passage from *In Search of Lost Time* when the narrator calls his grandmother. He describes the miracle of the other person's presence thanks to this device that abolishes the distance between the city of Paris and the town of Doncières, but also the feeling of absence due to this dissociation between a voice and an invisible speaking body:

> How often have I been unable to listen without anguish, as though, confronted by the impossibility of seeing, except after long hours of travel, her whose voice has been so close to my ear, I felt more clearly the sham and illusion of meetings apparently most pleasant, and at what a distance

1. See in particular: Jesse Dylan McCarthy, "Proust au téléphone," *Transposition* 6 (2016): https://journals.openedition.org/transposition/1491#bodyftn17

> we may be from the persons we love at the moment when it seems that we have only to stretch out our hand to seize and hold them. A real presence indeed that voice so near — in actual separation! But a premonition also of an eternal separation![2]

The singular beauty of these reflections on the presence/absence of a loved one whose voice can only be heard thanks to the telephone in fact participates in a spectral imaginary that became widespread with the arrival of these devices that gave sounds autonomy. The acousmatic voice, detached from its emitting mouth and expressing face, is listened to differently and takes on a tonality from beyond the grave. From the earliest days of the telephone, commentators have thus been divided between a sense of an amazement at synchronous communication with persons far away and of the irreality of a voice that seems to come from some hinter-world, or indeed from the beyond. This little mythology of absence and ghosts linked to the use of new devices for reproduction (photography) and transmission (telephony) has inspired a good number of literary fictions. What matters here in our underscoring a revolution in listening is the autonomy of sound. The annoyance caused by a bad telephone connection reminds the listener that they are in touch with sounds and not just the magic of a voice. Switchboard operators could interrupt a call, or the receiver might transmit calls other than the intended one, such that the device itself, with its adventitious sounds, would impose a sonic environment. Technological materiality fractured the illusion of presence/absence and shattered the sacrality of voices from the beyond, whether God's, Hamlet's father's, or the deceased's, leaving the listener with the profane crackling of the telephone line.

2. Marcel Proust, *The Guermantes Way* (trans. C. K. Scott Moncrieff; Yale University Press, 2018), 141–42.

Following this movement toward sonic autonomization thanks to the medium of the telephone, the voice exited its familiar landscapes associated with physiognomic expressions. As Proust said, it was "decanted," which is why he had the impression of discovering his grandmother's voice as though he had never heard it before:

> I heard the voice that I supposed myself, mistakenly, to know so well; for always until then, every time that my grandmother had talked to me, I had been accustomed to follow what she was saying on the open score of her face, in which the eyes figured so largely; but I was hearing her voice itself this afternoon for the first time.[3]

The voice, once decanted, is then heard for itself and associated with "scores" other than expression or the grammar of feelings. This word *score*, borrowed from music, sets out the staff along which affects, images, bodies, as well as sounds are composed among themselves. The voice, because it has become an autonomous sound, can be accompanied by realia other than lineaments and can take its place in new soundscapes. Such is the power of acousmatic sound to become available for arrangements that are neither natural nor familiar.

The materiality of sound and its new maneuverability due to telephonic devices has encouraged arrangements between voices and bodies previously unheard of. Our relation to words and to their meanings is changed by the act of putting the receiver over one's ear, of playing more or less freely with the proximity of the incoming voice to let it enter more deeply or to keep it at a distance and so as part of the sonic environment. A whole imaginary of sound develops with new devices like the telephone or gramophone, which the media theorist Friedrich Kittler

3. *Ibid.*, 142.

has been able to detect by studying the phantasmagorias that came out of these technological modernities.[4] The world itself and the human body become soundscapes, so long as we find devices that can make them audible. Kittler thus discusses a text by Rilke, "Primal Sound," in which the grooves of a skull might be made to give off sound using a gramophone needle. Everything becomes sonic and composable thanks to this trust in acoustic machines and devices that allowed us to capture voices and sounds, to transmit them using telephone receivers, gramophone horns, or speakers, to modulate them in space, and to change the way in which we listened to them. Far from being reducible to an improvement in the relations between individuals who could communicate more easily, the use of the telephone broke the order of words and the identity of speakers.[5] This new sonic device called into question the relation of the speaking subject to its voice, for the author of the voice and its location become dependent on the trust given to the sonic material that reaches the ear of the receiving subject. It also renews philosophical inquiries, as, for example, the meaning of a call: What does it mean to answer the phone, to take a call, to get cut off, etc.? And all this through the lens of a reflection on responsibility: To be called by someone unknown, to enter into contact with someone far off, to receive a call for help — these are

4. Friedrich A. Kittler, *Gramophone, Film, Typewriter* (trans. Geoffrey Winthrop-Young and Michael Wutz; Stanford University Press, 1999).
5. In keeping with Kittler, Avital Ronell focused her attention on the telephone and showed its philosophical impact: "Why the telephone? In some ways it was the cleanest way to reach the regime of any number of metaphysical certitudes. It destabilizes the identity of self and other, subject and thing, it abolishes the originariness of site; it undermines the authority of the Book and constantly menaces the existence of literature." *The Telephone Book: Technology — Schizophrenia — Electric Speech* (University of Nebraska Press, 1989), 9.

situations that resonate with ethical questions and that engage problems of relationship, lack, and summons with new stakes.

The acousmatic experience that results from the use of the telephone provoked philosophical and psychic transferences onto the device as a sonic object. The fact that the voice becomes almost materialized in the receiver — that synecdoche of the other's body one could play with without seeing it or being seen by it — alters the intersubjective relation. Jean Cocteau's 1929 play *The Human Voice* demonstrates how the telephone can transform into a transferential object, playing the role of fetish. A woman, alone on stage, speaks with her lover who has left her. The connection is often faulty, as in the situation described by Proust between the narrator and his grandmother, such that this woman must constantly call her interlocutor back to revive him in the device she holds in her hands, addressing him with beseeching "*Darling!*"s. The lover's voice, inaudible to the audience, becomes so for the forsaken character as well when there are intermittencies in the transmission due to technical failures, and these intermittencies put into even starker relief the darling object, the telephone, and its fetishistic use available to fantasies and anxieties. It solicits an energetic and libidinal expenditure that Cocteau had mischievously suggested in his preface: "Not only is the telephone sometimes more dangerous than a revolver, but also its meandering wire saps our strength." The character's gestures with the telephone embody this erotic charge: Her hand ceaselessly picks up and puts down the device; she hangs up and picks up in rhythm with its rings and voices — her lover's and the operator's. She associates the gloves of her beloved with the telephone handset, wraps the cord around her neck, and ends up lying on the bed hugging the device in her arms.

Many psychoanalytic readings have succeeded in clarifying this use of a device that joins ear and mouth. What interests us here concerns the dissociation of the voice and its speaking subject, the technological autonomization of sound, and the composable dimension of the voice as sound resulting from this acoustic device. Indeed the telephone irrupted not only into literature but also into music, as in the adaptation of Cocteau's play by Francis Poulenc who composed a *tragédie lyrique* from it in 1959, and into film, which has treated the telephone as far more than a motif, transforming it, with extraordinarily inventive richness, into a driving element of narrative.[6] The field of Media Studies has investigated the irruption of acoustic devices into modern society, and what we observe here is precisely the role they have played as experiments in thought and creation. They have indeed changed our ways of thinking, speaking, and writing. We shall support this hypothesis with three examples — Jean-Paul Sartre, Roland Barthes, and Samuel Beckett — based on their use of the telephone, radio, tape recorder, and megaphone. All three were music lovers, and all three were particularly sensitive to the question of the ear.

Before showing the changes new sonic devices made to these thinking voices, let us recall that the unity of a writer's "voice" or "style" is an illusion. The identification of a writer by the timbre of their voice perceptible in all of their writings obscures the existence of any number of constructed sonic components. A writer uses many voices and composes various soundscapes depending on circumstances. Unlike the dog from the Pathé Marconi advertisement who recognizes the voice of its master in the

6. Almodovar, in his 1987 *La lei del deseo*, used a scene from *The Human Voice* as an homage to the arrival of the telephone on the scene of desire.

gramophone, we hear multiple sonorities that writers adopt thanks to the acoustic devices they experimented with. The example of Sartre speaks to this rather loudly, as long as we reread his texts with our ears, discovering in them an author who is at once polygraphic and polyphonic. Indeed, Sartre never stopped trying out different genres and styles of writing, and the reasons for his choices were linked to particular acoustics.

Microphone thoughts

We should always investigate the sonic environments that predispose a thinker or writer's choices. Why does a creator suddenly decide to devote themselves to an entirely new creative genre, just as Sartre did, who, after writing novels and philosophical essays for fifteen years, suddenly devoted himself to theater? The usual answers often remain literary or ideological. They consist in pointing out the interest that Sartre discovered in certain theatrical works, such as the plays of Jean Giraudoux, which included sophisticated adaptations of Greek myths that Sartre would imitate in his first efforts. Encounters with directors, like Charles Dullin, can also explain Sartre's new dramaturgical infatuation. Sartre himself gave ideological explanation, telling how he appreciated the "collective" work of theatrical creation, as opposed to the solitude of writing, and how he strove to conceive great modern, political myths for the theater. Nevertheless, Sartre's conversion to theater has its origin in an exact, datable experience: In 1940, while prisoner in a Stalag in Germany, he found himself asked to participate in a Christmas show, for which he decided to compose a Nativity play. *Bariona, or the Son of Thunder* is not one of the works that Sartre reserved for his dramaturgical legacy; it was, however, decisive in his choice to devote himself to dramatic writing. Beyond any interpretation of the meaning of the play — its reference to Christianity, its emphasis on birth, the message of hope it sent to its audience of prisoners — the device that Sartre was experimenting with gave him access to a new dimension of speech. He hadn't, of course, waited until he was thirty-five to discover the theater, but, in these circumstances, he experienced its acoustic power. The lines he wrote for his characters and actors, who were his fellow prisoners (he himself played the role of the magus Balthazar), are directly spoken on stage and toward the audience. Sartre implemented synchronous speech, in direct contact with the listeners, which became a frontal acoustics allowing him to be "heard" in every sense of the word. Upon returning to Paris, though he continued his philosophical and novelistic work, he again undertook the writing of plays to rediscover that orality and direct address. *The Flies*, for example, is in the same vein as *Bariona*. The author's voice was no longer limited to intransitive writing: It carried far and instantly to multiple ears. A few years later, upon the Liberation, Sartre would find this taste for public and synchronous speech again thanks to the radio, understood as an acousmatic device giving such speech its widest diffusion.

The active role played by the radio makes it more than just a means of transmission, becoming a veritable character who insinuates itself into the privacy of its listeners' homes, just as Sartre had already highlighted in his novel *The Reprieve*, written between 1943 and 1944. This text undergoes maximal narrative fragmentation when Hitler's speech from 26 September 1938 gets broadcast through radio sets found across rather diverse social milieus. A multiplicity of points of view — or rather points of listening — gives the reader the illusion of simultaneously circulating through a myriad of places and the myriad consciousnesses of the listeners who hang on every word from this voice that would upheave so many lives and usher them into History. The radio is indeed the instrument that allowed Sartre to apply the technique of simultaneism, the model for which had been provided by the American writer John Dos Passos: Echoing the loudspeaker, which totalitarianisms — fascism, Nazism, and communism — made such extensive use to gather crowds and sonically manipulate the people, the radio dispenses with the physical presence of its listeners and infiltrates their ears to the very intimacy of their private lives. The Liberation provided Sartre the opportunity to use the microphone, not only during his lectures on existentialism, but also, in particular, during his weekly opinion pieces for the national radio in 1947. In these, he adopted a rather polemical tone, hostile to De Gaulle's party, and he sought to address his listeners directly. This political investment in the medium of radio differed radically from its use by Gaston Bachelard, who described it in a 1949 lecture as a waking dream that allows unconscious minds to commune.[7]

The experience of these various acoustic devices and the search for an at once maximal and synchronous auditory reception changed Sartre's writing and thinking. The orality he then put into practice, in theater and especially on the radio, led him to adopt assertive phrases, to choose rhetorical devices with striking rhythm, often antitheses, and to use a voice broken up by syncopations. Here the link between writing, style, inspiration, the development of thought, and the use of sound is evident; it only takes lending a little ear, even when reading, to recognize that an altered voice breathes rhythm into his sentences and reflections. Listening to Sartre's lectures and radio broadcasts

7. Gaston Bachelard, "La radio comme possibilité de rêve éveillé." https://www.franceculture.fr/emissions/les-nuits-de-france-culture/gaston-bachelard-la-radio-comme-possibilite-de-reve-eveille

allows us to read the texts he wrote at the same time for *Les Temps modernes* differently. His manifesto for an engaged literature, *What is Literature?*, which made him famous though at the cost of caricaturing him, develops like a speech delivered from a rostrum. It is a discourse of rhetorical effects, short, sometimes non-verbal sentences, and constant interlocutions through which Sartre sets up a theater of speaking positions. *No, we do not want ...*, *And why?...*, *They are going to invoke ...*, *I reply that ...*, *Which is to say never ...*, *It is easy to say ....* Sartre the rhetorician has in mind to enter a multitude of ears, to imprint a multitude of eardrums. His thinking sometimes becomes simplistic for this, relying on strictly binary oppositions, such as the transparency/opacity of language, or prose/poetry, which was the most famous of these oppositions. Sartre wrote with a microphone. And, at the same time, he theorized the necessity of addressing an audience, offering chapters on "For whom do we write?" or "The Writer's Situation in 1947," even though, as he would later acknowledge, he was writing at that time against himself in strained, over-blown, trumpeting language.

A dominant acoustic environment with its soundscapes can thus strongly motivate writing and thinking (for thought is forged directly from words and sounds). For all that, it remains compatible with different devices, as evidenced by Sartre's writings, which adopt several voices. The voice he developed during the post-war period within the spectrum of radio broadcasting remained compatible with other registers, notably those of the *flâneur* poetically describing the streets and crowds of New York City, or, later, cities in Italy. In these texts linked to his travels, sound is present, but in an immersive way, as when he describes the noises and vibrations he feels in his own body when a truck or subway passes by. His voice is filled with these sonic environments, whose waves he tries to transmit. On the other hand, his political texts are actively proclaimed in the very breath of the utterance and are constructed according to an intentional acoustics, arranged for interlocution. Sartre would always use contradictory acoustics, in a contemporary way, with incomparable voices. It was so in his public engagements, where he handled the microphone and played with his amplified voice, just as it was at home, in private, where he recorded himself singing with his daughter, whether eighteenth-century Baroque songs, twentieth-century opera arias, or melodies by Gabriel Fauré. At the end of his life, blindness limited him to dialogue, which engaged him in another form of thought, conditioned in its development by relations of voices. Dialogue's modes of affirmation and sites for improvisation and the interlocutors' adaptation to the tones of the other modify speech completely, as evidenced in Sartre's conversations with Benny Lévy, his last intellectual companion. Listening to such sonic determination of thought is made possible by the presence of a "device" that entered the scene in the theater of our minds: the magnetic tape recorder.

The democratization of the tape recorder introduced uses of sound that transformed the relation of listeners to voices and noises, which became multipurpose, playful objects. While the device was used as early as the 1930s for broadcasting propaganda speeches over the radio, it became available to the general public after World War II, entering homes and then, more broadly, popular culture. Films showed its dramatic and psychological resources through the great many narrative resources it offered, as with the dictaphone in Billy Wilder's 1944 *Double Indemnity* or the tapes that archive, reveal, trap, and betray in the works of our greatest filmmakers.

Samuel Fuller's 1964 *The Naked Kiss* magnifies, in a short scene, its functions of remembrance and revelation: The main character, a schoolteacher who has found the ideal husband, surprises him in the act of listening to a tape recorder playing a song she had her little students sing, and she suddenly understands that he is a pedophile. She then kills him with a telephone receiver, "ringing him," as it were — *à coup de téléphone*, literally 'with a strike of the telephone' — the device for communication transformed into an instrument of murder. The tape recorder acts doubly in this scene: It stimulates the man's repeated masturbation as he replays the tape of children's voices; and it summons the woman's memory who then understands the tape's acousmatic reality and infers child molestation.

From its archival function to the pleasure of repetition, the tape recorder, with its spools and tapes and buttons, went beyond its status as a recording device to become a multifunctional object and even a character in its own right. It played a major role in two theater pieces from the late 1950s: Beckett's *Krapp's Last Tape* and Sartre's *The Condemned of Altona* (aka. *Loser Wins*). In the last scene of *The Condemned*, the characters have disappeared and there is nothing left on the deserted stage other than spools that play the last speech of Frantz, the accursed representation of Nazi Germany, who has gone off to commit suicide with his father. The emphatic speech of this last will and testament bequeathing the tragic inheritance of the last century is tantamount to sonic testimony addressed to the auditory memory of those who survived. Beckett's use of the device, on the other hand, is much more inventive. Even if we could always find some politico-historical interpretation for this 1958 play, from the strict perspective of sound studies Beckett's analysis demonstrates the tape recorder's reflexive power regarding the voice and sound.

The play focuses on a man facing a tape recorder and numerous cardboard boxes containing reels of tape. Following a serial protocol, he selects the reels in order to listen to recordings he has made and which appear to be a diary of his past life. This sets up a sort of dialogue, composed of echoes, repetitions, and a dissociation between the character and his recorded voice. He listens, then records again; he comments on his past speeches, rewinds, and multiplies the mise en abyme of temporal strata. This gestural and oral choreography with the device diverts the tape recorder from its ostensible archival function.

Recording becomes intransitive: It no longer aims to fix the present or the past, but establishes a game of reflexive listening, confusing the voice emitted and the voice heard. The relation of a speaking subject to the microphone and to listening to their recorded voice indeed implies a singular reflexive experience, distinct from reflection in the mirror. *Hearing oneself* (*s'entendre*) is not based on self-objectification but rather produces detachment, for the recognition of the voice emitted and the voice listened to does not come about harmoniously. We do not hear ourselves as others hear us. In *The Human Condition* (aka. *Man's Fate*), André Malraux described his character Kyo's feeling of strangeness at not recognizing his recorded voice and has him explain it to his interlocutor thus: "We hear the voices of others with our ears. — *And our own?* — With our throats, for you can hear your own voice with your own ears stopped."[8] Beckett, as we noted above concerning accents, did not like his own voice and refused to be recorded. There are almost no recordings of Beckett speaking, only a speech accepting an award in Italy and a somewhat secretly recorded interview.

8. André Malraux, *Man's Fate* (trans. Haakon M. Chevalier; The Modern Library, 1934), 48.

Several psychological explanations have been given, in particular relating to his slight lisp, but the most important would be the impossible reflexivity that derails the subject toward a non-expressive, de-subjectified voice.[9] Experience with the tape recorder leads to listening to oneself as an other; it brings out the voice of the inner self and gives it an intriguing strangeness through its very familiarity. It dives directly into the question of the subject, its reflexivity and its recognition.

Who is thinking when I hear myself thinking with this voice that is mine yet that I do not fully recognize? The use of the tape recorder has inspired many reflections on the authority of the voice and on the impossible coincidence of the self to itself. The voice, which often passes for the marker of singularity when it travels through devices like the telephone, microphone, or tape recorder, becomes a sonic material whose identity is metastable. To be precise, it becomes sound once again, as it makes its sonic materiality heard and not just the mark of some speaking subject. This dissociative effect of self-recording is manifest for the voice, but also for any production of sound, notably music. Recording oneself playing music also induces a full spectrum of feelings, thoughts, and behaviors related to strangeness and auto-affection. Roland Barthes, like Beckett, did not like his own voice, even though he had worked on it for singing. He regularly recorded himself, however, playing piano. Such a project can be pedagogical, insofar as it allows one to hear the weaknesses of one's own playing by means of an external listening.

9. Beckett would again use a tape recorder in one of his television plays, the 1975 *Ghost Trio*. Playing with and against references to Beethoven's trio, from which he used the second movement, *Largo assai ed espressivo*, Beckett articulated camera movements according to its musical measures, treating them without expression. The character holding the tape recorder playing this music bends over it little by little.

Still, the ease of recording, made possible by the portable tape recorder, led amateurs such as Barthes or Sartre to record themselves for other reasons, or indeed other pleasures. The hundred or so hours that Sartre recorded on magnetic tapes to preserve his musical moments with his daughter — singing or playing the piano or the flute — were not just for learning. They were part of taking pleasure in repetition and shared listening. Barthes took intellectual pains to question this practice of self-recording, which he too did, like Sartre, but in solitude.

In *Roland Barthes by Roland Barthes*, he devoted one of his reflections to it, aptly named "Coincidence." Contrary to the distance caused by listening to one's own voice, here there is a sort of self-recognition that seems to come about when the instrumentalist listens to himself. Then an immanent pleasure from bonding the self to itself gets played out thanks to the music:

> I record myself playing the piano: initially, out of curiosity to *hear myself*; but very soon I no longer hear myself; what I hear is, however pretentious it may seem to say so, the *Dasein* of Bach and of Schumann, the pure materiality of their music; because it is my utterance, the predicate loses all pertinence; on the other hand, paradoxically, if I listen to Horowitz or Richter, a thousand adjectives come to mind: I hear *them* and not Bach or Schumann. — What is it that happens? When I listen to myself *having played* — after an initial moment of lucidity in which I perceive one by one the mistakes I have made — there occurs a kind of rare coincidence: the past of my playing coincides with the present of my listening, and in this coincidence, commentary is abolished: there remains nothing but the music

> (of course what remains is not at all the 'truth' of the text, as if I had rediscovered the 'true' Schumann or the 'true' Bach).[10]

The description of this experience is ambivalent, for it brings out an equivalence between Barthes's playing and the music of Bach or Schumann, as if any mediation had vanished, as if there were no interpretation but the pure presence of a musical work. The experience of immediacy comes from Barthes rejection of listening to professional musicians and explains his taste for self-recording, for he recognizes in it his own relation to music: He hears the Bach or Schumann that he loves, which is to say himself playing Bach or Schumann. Coincidence thus defines less the relation of piano playing to a composer's score than it does the pleasure, the *jouissance* of an intimate relation between listening and the body playing. When Barthes listened to himself playing, he was touched by the musical play produced by his hands; he touched himself anew — he auto-affected himself — through the ear. This coincidence is put into practice between him and himself, more than between him and the piece of music. Barthes thereby diverted analysis of sonic reflexivity toward an erotics of self-listening: a musical self from which we derive all the more pleasure when it melds into the materiality of sound. It is less that the dissociation of the subject leads to an ordeal of strangeness than that it procures a quasi-masturbatory pleasure carried away by indeterminacy: *It* can be played ...; *it* can be listened to ...; *it* has a beat. Barthes sometimes gave erotic descriptions of musical pleasure:

10. Roland Barthes, *Roland Barthes by Roland Barthes* (trans. Richard Howard; University of California Press, 1977), 55–56.

"What is required is that *it beat* inside the body, against the temple, in the genitals, in the belly, against the skin from the inside ...."[11]

The magnetic tape recorder, made available to lovers of sound, has thus furnished us with philosophical, aesthetic, and psychic resources. The manipulations it allows, with the back and forth of its reels and the convenience of repeat play, have modified the relation that subjects have to their own voices, their sonic emissions, and their acoustic environments. Modern practices brought about by the telephone, the microphone, and the tape recorder are therefore not limited to technological progress, but have transformed the very meaning of reflection and communication. Thinkers like Sartre conceived new modes of interlocution and a way of thinking conditioned by acoustic milieus. Beckett's inventiveness also owes much to them, for he furthered his work on language, breath, and sound by experimenting with them. And Barthes drew inspiration from them to develop a number of ideas that were at once semiotic and phenomenological based on the relation of the body to rhythms and sounds. These examples, among many others, bear witness to the fact that thinking and creating are coupled to sonic milieus and that the quality of a thinker or creator is doubtless measured by the acuity of their listening and their ability to mix and edit the sounds that surround them.

11. Roland Barthes, "Rasch" (in *The Responsibility of Forms*, trans. Richard Howard; Hill and Wang, 1985), 302. Translation modified.

Might hearing be *the* philosophical sense par excellence? To hear well is to think well. Nietzsche maintained as much against the tradition of seeing well, and he judged the quality of a philosophy on the basis of its auditory acuity. Playing and listening to music naturally supported the exercise of reflection:

> A better musician, a better listener. [...] Has it been noticed that music liberates the spirit? gives wings to thought? that one becomes more of a philosopher the more one becomes a musician?[1]

Being a musician is not reducible to knowing music, but above all means knowing how to listen and thereby how to access the "between the lines" of reality. Still, to reach this sonic dimension, one must put oneself in a position to hear, to pick out the noises and music of the world. Where the passive listener receives sounds indistinctly, the philosophical listener actively discerns them and knows how to best arrange them. A good thinker will know how to choose their acoustic milieu as a mental device for such arrangements. The construction of thought indeed resembles sound mixing whereby sounds, noises, and voices are organized to give them a coherent dynamic. This sonic material preexists the development of ideas and arguments, as one never thinks from nothing, but against the background brouhaha of voices. Soundtracks may already be present, especially with established voices, pre-recorded, as fixed sounds. They are then edited when it comes time for the formal elaboration of philosophical discourse. The supposed silence of thought is populated with dead voices murmuring in the memory of language. What an original philosophy then does is concern itself with forging a voice for itself

1. Friedrich Nietzsche, *The Birth of Tragedy* and *The Case of Wagner* (trans. Walter Kaufmann; Vintage, 1967), 157–58.

in this whispering of dead voices. The thinking subject must compose with those voices that breathe into it preformed sonic compounds, which suggest certain intonations, volumes, and rhythms.

Soundtracks of philosophical thought

A thinker always works from such an ensemble of voices, which they arrange and transform. As modern as this portrait of philosophical activity as a sound mixing board may seem, it defines practices as old as those of Plato, who gathered vocal sources surrounding Socrates to balance, or rather to isolate the philosophical soundtrack par excellence, one that makes the voice of truth heard amid the cacophony of opinions. Whether in direct dialogue with an adversary or intertwined with the speech of several disciples, Socrates's voice, as mixed by Plato, imposes itself with different balances and intensities: It triumphs in glory at the end of the text; or it persists like a soft basso continuo while the other voices gradually fade out. Such orality is not reserved for works in theatrical form; the mixing of voices can also be heard in writings with univocal enunciation. Michel de Montaigne's *Essays* offer the finest example. There Montaigne is in constant dialogue with the Ancients, weaving his own voice over theirs, quoting them as though they were present, telling their stories, debating with them. As we noted above, Montaigne privileges hearing over sight, putting conversation above all other activities. The library where he wrote the *Essays*, withdrawn from the political world, was a sound box for these voices from other times, sometimes engraved on the very beams of this solitary space that filled with echoes.

Montaigne's own voice was mixed insofar as it changed over the course of writing, and editions of the Bordeaux copy of the *Essays* have conserved the strata of those moments where he made additions, contradicted himself, or commented on his previous thinking, refusing to erase the trace of his past voices. There are three soundtracks, marked by the letters *A*, *B*, and *C*, which get edited together in a final version, allowing us to hear three philosophical voices. This is the case, for example, with his reflections on death, which were in dialogue as they evolved over time. They begin in an imperious, heroic voice, with Montaigne the Stoic using imperatives to recommend ceaseless thinking about our final fate:

> Let us have nothing on our minds as often as death. At every moment let us picture it in our imagination in all its aspects. [...] And there upon let us tense ourselves and let us make an effort.[2]

A decade and a half later, with old age at work on his body, Montaigne preferred to extol an art of living that focused on the present and did not distract itself with funereal thoughts. Contradicting his initial claim, he would later observe: "But it seems to me that death is indeed the end, but not therefore the goal, of life; it is its finish, its extremity, but not therefore its object."[3] This is in fact an entirely different voice heard at the end of the *Essays*, one that is more personal, less clear-cut. It accords with temperaments and voices other than those of the illustrious, like the voices of the peasants whom Montaigne saw die with dignity without ever having read Seneca. Montaigne's voice, while making its uniqueness in the history of philosophy heard, is intrinsically polyphonic, and the continual

2. Montaigne, *Essays* (trans. Donald Frame; Stanford University Press, 1958), 1.20, 60. Translation modified.
3. *Ibid.*, 3.12, 805.

stichting he did to his text is part of a complex sound mixing he used to regulate its frequencies according to an art of recording entirely his own.

Observing the acoustic arrangements in which thought experiments take place can be highly rewarding. Often dramatized by biographers, these places and moments are closely linked to sonic environments, like the convent or cell of a solitary thinker. They are arranged like stages where a vocation is produced, whether it is a call to transcendence or a word that slips into a soundproof room. Access to divine speech, to the Voice of voices, thus comes about through a negative acoustic, which allows for the erasure of all sounds in order to give the divine voice its greatest amplitude. The space of prayer and meditation is not a void; on the contrary, it is rich in the divine presence; it is the "plenitude" of pure sound. The moment of intellectual revelation also implies, for many philosophers, a particular acoustic. Consider the young Descartes as he involuntarily received the vocation to philosophy in a small heated room he lived in at Neuburg called a *poêle*, 'stove'. There he was visited by three dreams which he interpreted as an invitation to consecrate himself to the search for truth. The second of these dreams was a sonic experience, associating the noise in the room with noise in the dream. Adrien Baillet, Descartes's first biographer, explained how the young man mistook the crackle of burning wood for a clap of thunder. This little confusion was then interpreted as a divine sign: The lightning had frightened the dreamer in order to inform him of his past sins and to indicate a new path, the sonic jolt giving this signal its greatest intensity. The simple cracking of the twigs being consumed, by the effect of acoustic amplification, was transformed into a soundtrack, mixed with the two other dreams and sketching out a whole new path for the soon-to-be philosopher who would then abandon his military career. The moment and the place for a reflection or a decision, what might also be called its setting, are of the utmost importance. And in this composite of circumstances and affinities, the sonic environment plays a major role. The confined atmosphere of a room — whether cell, library, or office — thereby allows us to hear the acoustic functioning of thought with its voices, its precise noises, and its silence.

The sonic environment in which we think, write, or read is not always perceptible, or, at least, we are not often aware of it. We discern it only when we take a step back in order to investigate what we are doing: What sounds accompany our thinking or our reading? Suddenly we understand that there are noises and melodies associated with these activities. Has their presence played an adventitious role? Has it left traces on the order of a motif or an ambience? Responses to these questions cannot be univocal, as situations differ greatly. Still, these questions deserve more precise formulation. Wittgenstein's analysis proves valuable here for avoiding facile generalizations and analogies. In the *Brown Book*, he asks himself what happens when we read a text and what formulations lead us to describe a particular atmosphere:

> When noticing this atmosphere I am in the situation of a man who is working in his room, reading, writing, speaking, etc., and who suddenly concentrates his attention on some soft uniform noise, such as one can almost always hear, particularly in a town (the dim noise resulting from all the various noises of the street, the sounds of wind, rain, workshops, etc.).

> We could imagine that this man might think that a particular noise was a common element of all the experiences he had in this room.[4]

Nevertheless, this noise is not necessarily identifiable, and it might have changed without the writer noticing. For all that, Wittgenstein observes that it would not be quite right to define such inattentive listening as a secondary experience that gets added to writing or reading. Rather it is more certainly a "composite experience" of variable cohesion: Such noise can play a decisive role, like a G note in a C-E-G chord; or it might instead be associative, orientating, diverting, or supporting our linguistic activity. It could accompany thinking, writing, or reading, like a humming that the thinking, writing, or reading subject cannot not objectively put their finger on.

The presence of sounds in the composition of thought is heard all the more as their dynamics are brought to bear over time, whether time spent writing or time spent walking. The sonic milieus outside confined rooms offer infinite philosophical resources to thinkers who take walks. The philosophical stroll provides an example: It engages the active posture of bodies in motion who, unlike those who remain seated or supine, join with the sonic vibrations of the world. Doubtless we must distinguish here between walks with several people like those of the Peripatetics who followed Aristotle, methodical walks along an invariable route like the one Kant took daily, and walks listening to things, ears open to chance encounters.[5] Rousseau was this last type of walker; he loved both solitude and immersing himself in the sounds of nature. The fifth walk

4. Ludwig Wittgenstein, *The Blue and Brown Books* (Harper Torchbooks, 1965), 167–68.
5. On the relation of thinking to walking, see Frédéric Gros, *A Philosophy of Walking* (trans. John Howe; Verso, 2023).

of his *Reveries of the Solitary Walker* is both a biographical meditation on the feeling of serenity he had while on St. Peter's Island in the middle of Lake Biel, Switzerland, and a philosophical reflection on happiness as fullness, absence of lack, immanence, conformity with the present. Like contemplatives, Rousseau sought silence and wanted to erase all artificial noises, which is to say those noises of civilization and its factitious pleasures. Still, this fading out of sounds did not aim for the absolute silence of a monastic cell; on the contrary, it allowed him to hear the sounds of nature. Rousseau's meditation is fully inscribed in a dynamic soundscape, defined through the selection and mixing of sounds that harmonize. The thinker could thus meditate "in a silence unbroken by any sound other than that of the cry of eagles, occasional birdsong, and the rumbling of streams cascading down the mountains."[6] His walk was a quest for the best moment and space that could be arranged for the perfect murmur, one that would most intensely manifest his feeling that every single thing participated in existence.

Rousseau indeed wandered about in order to reach the best spots for listening, and, when evening came, he would come down from the island to sit on its lakeshore and be filled by a soundscape that absorbed him whole, without exteriority:

> There, the sound of the waves and the movement of the water, gripping my senses and ridding my soul of all other agitation, plunged it into a delicious reverie, in the course of which night often fell without my noticing and took me by surprise. The ebb and flow of the water and its continuous yet constantly varying sound, ever breaking against my ears and my eyes, took the place of the movements inside

6. Jean-Jacques Rousseau, *Reveries of the Solitary Walker* (trans. Russell Goulbourne; Oxford University Press, 2011), 49.

> me that reverie did away with and were enough to make me pleasantly aware of my existence, without my having to take the trouble to think."[7]

With Rousseau, the unity of the self is not acquired by the elimination of sensation, but, on the contrary, through an attentive hearing of the sonic world. Sometimes he walked, sometimes he napped in a boat drifting on the lake, and sometimes he sat at the edge of a river or stream and listened to the murmur of water over stone. Doubtless such experiences relate more to meditation than to reflection, the mind's transcendent activity giving way to the subject's immanent experience of being in conformity with nature. Rousseau recalls the little thoughts that came to his mind on seeing shimmering waters, like his reflections on the instability of things. And yet he allowed sounds to carry him away more than images; he became one with the waves, joining the surrounding vibrations and melding into the uniform movement of these sounds that transform the world into a vast lullaby. A soundscape delimited by the active listening of a walker inclined toward the best acoustics could thus become a sonic environment in which the contemplative listener could abandon their exteriority and attain a sense of completeness that is both simultaneously active and passive and, more broadly, participative. The subject is at once focused on themselves, without distraction, and immersed in a peaceful nature. This is a happiness achieved through two sonic processes: first, identifying and mixing sounds; and, then, immersive listening in the vibratory continuum thus captured.

Taking a walk in a sonic milieu can also sustain an active and reflective mind. While immersion may bring with it a pleasure that is as sensual as it is meditative, their

7. *Ibid.*, 54.

association offers another mode of listening as well, one comprising analysis, provocation, and digression. Walking, listening, and thinking go together according to a temporal dynamic that brings soundtracks — voices, noises, and melodies — together. Associating an idea, an argument, or a philosophical intention with some sonic milieu is easily done when one articulates the rhythm of one's step, its weight and speed along a certain path. The composition of a soundscape is based on affinities between various acoustic elements, whether the sound of pebbles underfoot, the beating of the heart, the breath of respiration, the rustling of leaves in the wind, or the thrumming of an engine, depending on how urban or rural the place being traversed is. The philosopher who most regularly evoked this sonic inspiration for his thinking is doubtless Nietzsche, that traveler (*Wanderer*) who claimed walking to be a necessary philosophical activity. According to him, thought only arises if one leaves the monastic cell, the classroom, or the academy to go on an adventure. Nietzsche indeed left the University of Basel, where he held a university position, and wandered through the Engadine and along the shores of the Mediterranean, far from his native Germany. The description of his philosophical inspirations, as we recalled above concerning his walk in the Silvaplana region, is tightly linked to sonic phenomena: Whether in Sils Maria, Nice, Eze, Genoa, Recoaro, Rome, Venice, or Turin, it is always a matter of voices, sounds, a particular melody, a piece of music, etc. His ideas — in particular of the eternal return — and his books are constructed from his shaping and mixing these sonic sources.

The politics of noises

The definition of thought as the mixing of sounds, whether in an enclosed space or out in the open, was formulated with a good deal of vivacity by a philosopher who influenced Nietzsche and was himself also a great lover of music: Arthur Schopenhauer. In a seemingly minor text, which composed part of his *Parerga and Paralipomena*, Schopenhauer asserted with some virulence that hearing is the criterion of mind, and he distinguished those who accept all noises without distinction from those who select from among them. In this text, titled "On Noise and Sounds," which was one of the supplements that Schopenhauer offered to the general public, he did not hesitate to provoke his readers by flaunting his insolent liberty. His reflections on listening took aim at the Germans, a people who were paradoxically musical yet who tolerated noises incompatible with thinking. While Schopenhauer described his ideal acoustic environment by contrast and inveighed against the din that perturbed his concentration, he also expanded his observations into an anthropology of listening and thereby pursued a reflection on sound, which he had already begun in his *The World as Will and Representation*, where he had remarked:

> I have actually thought for some time that the quantity of noise someone can tolerate is in inverse proportion to his mental powers, and can be regarded as an approximate measure of these. And so when I hear a dog left to bark for hours on end in the courtyard of a house, I already know what to think about the mental abilities of the inhabitants. Anyone who has a habit of slamming doors instead of

> closing them by hand, or who allows this in their house, does not simply have bad manners but is crude and narrowminded.[8]

The noises that bothered Schopenhauer relate to interruption: They rupture the sonic milieu of his thought. One can thus distinguish between two types of thinker in the "history of philosophy": those thinkers who privileged continuity and those who sought rupture. The former construct their thought according to a flow, a temporality at once compact and fluid, which comes about on its own. The latter establish their ideas on the cut, the syncope, the offbeat. Aristotle, Spinoza, Bergson, and Deleuze belong to the first group; Plato, Descartes, and Sartre to the second. In his description of a sonic milieu that favored the mind, Schopenhauer extolled the continuous concentration of thinking, which nothing should interrupt. Intrusive sounds enraged him; they cut him off, short-circuiting him.[9] Among these sounds, the worst, which would rip apart a thinker's soundscape, was the coachman's whip: "Hammer blows, dogs barking and the screaming of children are appalling, but only the crack of a whip is the real murderer of thoughts."[10] Schopenhauer the philosopher-acoustician argues here that the act of cracking a whip is functionally useless, for, in reality, it is just noise for noise's sake. Horses get used to it, and they could easily react to and obey much quieter sounds: Like dogs and canaries,

8. Arthur Schopenhauer, *The World as Will and Representation* Vol. 2 (trans. Judith Norman, Alistair Welchman, and Christopher Janaway; Cambridge University Press, 2018), 34.
9. When responding to the word *animal* during his *Abécédaire* (*Alphabet Book*), Gilles Deleuze confessed his abhorrence at barking, "the stupidest of cries [...] the shame of the animal kingdom."
10. Arthur Schopenhauer, "On Noise and Sounds," in *Parerga and Paralipomena* Vol. 2 (trans. Adrian Del Caro; Cambridge University Press, 2015), 576.

Schopenhauer makes clear, horses have rather acute hearing. Cracking a whip merely flatters the coarseness of base minds, who love a racket. That coachmen sometimes use their whip with no horses around only proves the point. Schopenhauer transforms this noise into a symbol of society's vindictive struggle against those finer minds who work with their heads and who need a homogenous sonic milieu to do so. His heroic mission against noise takes on somewhat excessive proportions in the name of a defense of philosophizing against the masses, who hate intellectual work. Schopenhauer even called for corporal punishments for noisy troublemakers as counter-violence on behalf of those who wished to preserve their sonic milieu. A veritable acoustic war was unleashed, which we could call a war of refined versus asinine ears. The form and quality of ears has certainly been a touchstone for sound minds: In his *An Essay Concerning Human Understanding*, John Locke had suggested trying to imagine humans with pointier ears to see whether we came to think of them instead as animals.

In this conflict between elevated and base minds, the ear is a thinker's weak point, exposing them to violence through the ear canal. In a hyperbolic and paranoid train of thought, Schopenhauer estimated the number of thoughts interrupted, and so destroyed, by whip cracks throughout human history. Modern technology is not in question here, for in every age, noisy people have assaulted thinkers who had more acute ears. So it was for the sixteenth-century painter and poet Bronzino, who wrote a poem against the noise of the streets. And even Juvenal in the second century railed against the din of the city in his *Satires.*[11] Too great a tolerance for such a racket has always been the sign of a base — or empty — mind. Schopenhauer thus called on nations to maintain a level of civilization by throttling noise and silencing those who would knock on doors or crack whips. Such recriminations might seem comical, yet, before Nietzsche, Schopenhauer considered hearing as the primary sense, through which the auditory nerve communicated directly to the innermost part of the brain. He observed that, indeed, great minds, like Kant, Goethe, and Jean Paul, arranged their lives according to their sonic milieus, while the stupid remained insensible to noise. One's relation to sound is thus a measure of intelligence, the quality of which is gauged, on Schopenhauer's account, according to how hearing gets tuned, or, we might say, according to how the sonic elements that compose an acoustic world get mixed. Thinking well means knowing how to compose the best sonic milieu for one's mind and to select its most advantageous sounds.

Schopenhauer's anger at the noises of society might stem from the elitism of refined minds, who know how to mix their own sonic milieu, but it also suggests a politics of sound, or at least a sociopolitical analysis of acoustic spaces and their balances. The war against noise has often had an anti-popular ring to it, the plebs beings associated with indistinct, coarse, raucous sounds. Still, this division, which remains at the level of volume, remains too simplistic. Noise aggression is not limited to irruptions or disturbances caused by the roaring masses; it is also part of a sonic hegemony of capitalist society that dominates people

11. Juvenal, *Satire* 3 (in *Juvenal and Persius*, trans. Susanna Morton Braund; Harvard University Press, 2004), 187: "Which lodgings allow you to rest, after all? You have to be very rich to get sleep in Rome. That's the source of the sickness. The continual traffic of carriages in the narrow twisting streets and the swearing of the drover when his herd has come to a halt would deprive a Drusus or the seals of sleep."

by channeling their listening. If, according to Schopenhauer, independent minds are those capable of selecting and mixing sounds, the imposition on an entire society of the same indistinct sonic atmosphere constitutes a power of domination. Those unable to mix sounds, or who believe they are choosing their sounds when they are only participating in the general sonic flow, are alienated by the sonorization of their individual and collective lives. Conversely, freedom gets defined as having the possibility to choose one's sounds.

A political philosophy must therefore consider the issue of sound mixing and each individual's availability to determine their acoustic milieu. While the proliferation of sources for sound and of ways to spread music readily gives us the illusion of such freedom, asserting of our musical tastes does not prevent there being a standardization of listening. For such is indeed the criterion of independence: not selecting one's favorite pieces, but being able to escape the constant sonorization of spaces. Today, it is difficult to escape *muzak*, the name for elevator music also heard in parking lots, restaurants, waiting rooms, etc. Thinking is less hindered by interruptive door slams than by the cloying permanence of mixed sounds. Or, at least, this hindrance operates differently from the disruption of individual sonic milieus: It instead keeps our minds in a pseudo-serenity or torpor that deprives them of identifying milieus more conducive to the exercise of their freedom of thought.

Philosophers of the Frankfurt School, in particular Adorno, figured out how to analyze this insidious submission of hearing. According to Adorno, who was both musician and musicologist, our mercantile and capitalist society had brought about a regression in listening. Through the reification of musical works, which had become entertainment products designed for consumer satisfaction, it had deprived listeners of their autonomy. It had equalized sonic forms through their reproduction and repetition; it had standardized listening to the point that it became the simple reception of the general sonic flow. One could whistle the melody of a Brahms symphony on the subway, or that of a pop song — a listener would no longer be able to differentiate these sounds. As market goods that could be consumed immediately, they are both reproducible and become faded into the sonic rite of capitalist society and its musical objects. For Adorno,

> the intensification of sound, which emphasizes the reified parts, takes on the character of a magical ritual, while all the mysteries of personality, inwardness, inspiration, and spontaneity, which emanate from the work itself, are banished by its reproduction.[12]

The commercial prescription of sounds, compatible with all the other standardized activities of society, has thereby eliminated independent listening, the kind of listening that knows how to discriminate between sounds and discover the transgressive power of a musical work. The consumer's ear is thus condemned to passivity: Even if it varies what it listens to, it no longer distinguishes between noise and music, between commodity and creation, between pleasure and enjoyment. The only antidote to this regression of listening, according to Adorno, can come from individuals who create a new type of music. This analysis, at once elitist and pessimistic, from a philosopher who believes he knows what kind of music can lead to social emancipation, has, whether we agree or not, the merit of showing how sonic milieus have a political

12. Theodor W. Adorno, "On the Fetish-Character in Music and the Regression of Listening" (in *Essays on Music*, trans. Susan H. Gillespie; University of California Press, 2002), 298. Translation modified.

dimension. It points out how one's way of listening, this "art of listening" whose renaissance Nietzsche had hoped for, is at the heart of thought. Being able to choose and mix the sounds that populate one's mind, discerning which sonic spaces allow or prohibit the expression of one's individuality and freedom — such are the political stakes of sound mixing.

The critique of noise — of invasive noise, the vulgar din, and modern brouhaha — often sounds a reactionary motif. It expresses nostalgia for a harmonious time or a silent space — of nature or the monastic cell — where an acoustic order once reigned, where the distribution of noises respected the comfort of well-educated ears, and everyone knew what volume not to exceed. This recrimination against the disastrous sonorization of society — electrified sounds, commercial music, the hustle and bustle of the streets, etc. — leads to the eulogizing of silent or natural milieus. It also leads to extolling music that allows one to escape the standardization of hearing, suggesting, against the general hubbub, a refuge in earlier music, or the hope of a radically new music. This refrain against noise is not, however, the apanage of conservatism, but also nourishes critiques of how sound is used by both totalitarianism and capitalism. What we retain most is its injunction to recognize the collective dimension of all listening. This politics of hearing engages an ecology of the sonic milieus we inhabit, not just our living spaces but also the languages we hear and speak.

We think by mixing sounds, for all thought is sonic, even if it claims silence as its privileged space. Philosophers who give primary importance to listening have thus emphasized this acoustic dimension and the more or less discreet presence of noises, voices, and melodies in their thinking. This sonic habitat, whether we call it a sonic milieu or soundscape, is habitually undervalued or misunderstood. Discovering it and recognizing its driving force in the formation of signs and ideas presupposes a *sonic ecology* that concerns both the auditory perception and apprehension of sounds in images, texts, and intellectual constructs. What, however, can the phrase "inhabiting sound" mean through these various perceptual and fictional experiences?

The notions of soundscape and sonic milieu may seem related, but they imply different conceptions of sound. To better grasp what we are talking about when using these expressions, we must open our ears and ask ourselves whether we can truly isolate sounds, whether we can frame them like a painting, whether we can trace their borders like objects. And when we hear sounds "in our head" without their coming to us from an external audition, what idea do we have of their nature? Are they comparable to the images of reality that consciousness apprehends? When we read and so come to "hear" a voice, a tune, or a noise, do such virtual or "fictional" sounds have the same qualities as real sounds? Such questions belong to a philosophy of perception, and, though that is not our goal here, we nevertheless need to clarify the meaning of sound in an "ecology of acoustics" in order to listen to, define, and describe the presence of sound both around us and in texts. The physics of sound alone cannot provide all the answers, insofar as it is the auditory consciousness that receives or produces sounds, which it does not simply perceive passively as objects entering through the ears. This auditory consciousness associates sounds with other perceptions, and even with affects, images, and thoughts. The resonance of a bell, for example, will be heard with more or less objectivity, as its vibration penetrates and affects the listener's body. The memory of this sound might become associated with memories and images of churches or temples specific to different religions and cultures. The time and place of its reverberation also strongly condition the way it is heard. Heard off in the distance or very close to our ears, this bell will not have the same sound, the same meaning, or the same effects. Depending on whether it ruptures an acoustic balance or harmonizes with other noises, it might itself constitute a soundscape. Affinities will then be constructed, composed of corresponding sensations and of what gets associated with its vibrations in our imagination.

Relational sound

We can distinguish two general conceptions of sound when approaching a sonic ecology: one defines its nature, and, more precisely, its physics; the other conceives sound in a relational way, through its contingencies. The former aims to objectify sound by analyzing the propagation of waves through spaces and materials. It might also seek to define the sonic objects composed by humans and understand their effects. Thus, in the nineteenth century, the physicist Hermann von Helmholtz had the ambition of analyzing hearing in humans and identifying the harmonics that give us a feeling of consonance or dissonance. The physicalist approach to sound has spread beyond the realm of science and come to interest composers who have turned their attention to sound as such, freed from any musical aesthetic. Thus, Pierre Schaeffer, who considered sound as a material, and so created "sound objects" (*objets sonores*) through various technical manipulations. And thus,

Iannis Xenakis, who conceived his compositions as the deployment of sonic masses through the space in which he immersed his listeners. When sound is analyzed as, thought of as, and composed as a material, it acquires independence, or at least an objectivity that allows one to define its contours, dynamics, and effects. Nevertheless, this preeminence of sound rests, perhaps, on an overvaluation of sound per se. Isolated, as though it existed by itself, sound gives the impression of constituting a world in its own right. And yet, when we speak of a sonic milieu or soundscape, we doubtless summon other components from among the spaces and dynamics we are sensitive to as listeners. A certain fetishism of sound — like the fetishism of music denounced by Adorno — has concealed sound's relations to other phenomena.

A relational approach allows us to define "sonic ecology" better as a new listening to the milieus in which we perceive or conceive sounds. Phenomenology has contributed to this approach, as we observed above with Merleau-Ponty and his *Phenomenology of Perception.* Merleau-Ponty investigated not only sound and auditory sensation, but also, above all, the consciousness of sound. The objective reality of sound then becomes less important than the manner in which it arises as a phenomenon. Still, by bracketing all judgment and understanding, consciousness does not reach any kernel of pure sound. It is itself engaged in perception, moving from consciousness of sound to sonic consciousness. And in particular, when it emits sounds, it becomes sonically auto-affected, as when speaking it speaks and hears itself. Its own body participates in the vibration it produces and receives, and it puts into motion all that surrounds it. Beyond phenomenology and its attachment to the notion of consciousness, we can define a sonic milieu as the set of relations that implicate sonic objects, their vibrations, their contexts, and the listeners who take them in. Other words too are pertinent for defining such relational acoustics, like sonic *atmosphere* or *ambience*. The word *environment*, as ecologists know, remains inadequate, for it keeps the subject at the center, heterogeneous from its surroundings. To be sure, the science of acoustics has been used in service of a better environmental politics, aiming to reduce the harms of certain frequencies and vibrations that pollute our ecosystems. Nevertheless, it resides on an objective conception of sound as external to its hearers. As the theorist of sonic ecology Makis Solomos has observed:

> We must therefore continue our attempts to conceptualize and search for new concepts that will allow us to consider the *inextricable links between the vibrating object, the milieu in which the vibration spreads and the subject who listens*.[1]

Beyond any objectivization of sound, conceptualizing sonic milieus requires apprehending the relational tissue that associates sound with other phenomena through contingent effects, which science cannot readily integrate.

Literature is doubtless more able to approach these sonic milieus, which function via the interplay of affinities, and to make them audible. The science of acoustics keeps to natural causation, and philosophy performs conceptual syntheses that bypass the particular dynamics of sonic relations. Literary texts, on the other hand, by their very textuality — their tissue, their fabric — intend to make these echoes audible, those remnants of sounds and voices that get articulated among numerous other elements

1. Makis Solomos, "From Sound to Sound Space, Sound Environment, Soundscape, Sound Milieu or Ambiance…," *Paragraph* 41.1 (2018): 95–109, 99.

of sensation and imagination. Among writers most attentive to the perception of sounds and to the sonic matter of writing, Pascal Quignard has, for some time, put forth reflections on and descriptions of sonic milieus. In his essays and stories, he emphasizes the immersion of consciousness in sound, all while preserving a position of exteriority that allows him to decipher the nature and effects, sometimes destructive, of this connaturality of bodies and sounds. Interest in sound, and not just musical sound, is embodied in the person of Simeon Pease Cheney, a musician who lived in New England in the nineteenth century, known for having transcribed birdsong even before Ravel or Messiaen had. Quignard's *In this Garden We Loved* describes Cheney's life, and he becomes an echo to Quignard's own auditory acuity, with Quignard observing that Cheney's recordings extended to ordinary noises as well:

> He noted the lapping of the rain on the pond. The clinking of the iron chain in the well knocking against that strange bell, the empty bucket, descending into the vertical shadow of the circle of stones [...] the crumpling of skirts, slips, dresses that come off the belly when their cords are loosened and fall heavily on the floor of the marital chamber. [...] Suddenly in the middle of the night, the urine of the woman you love trickling into the large earthenware chamber pot after she removed the wooden lid in the recess of the wall.[2]

The enumeration of noises that capture the composer's attention, as imagined by Quignard, integrates surrounding sounds to construct them into a landscape and associate them with visual and tactile perceptions, as well as feelings and desires. The triviality of these noises allows him to avoid musical metaphors, which would be too facile,

2. Pascal Quignard, *Dans ce jardin qu'on aimait* (Grasset, 2017), 62–63.

allowing him instead to hear "airs" being composed — not melodies, but sonic affinities that give the impression of an ordered association among sounds while they remain contingent, arising randomly. Circumstances — which is to say the more or less random encounter of sonic objects with the ears that hear them and the milieu in which they develop and associate — take on an unexpected coherence, as though the relations they offer experience arose out of necessity. The musician transcribes them, the writer decyphers them and recomposes them in his own way, transforming his text into a musical score. Writing allows us to hear the relations that sounds maintain with nature and with the lives of others, their perceptions, feelings, and imaginations.

"There are no soundscapes," Quignard declared in his *The Hatred of Music*,[3] but this was only to underline the impossible gap between listeners and the sounds that surround them, unlike spectators in front of a painting. This observation of an immersive presence is at the foundation of a philosophical, indeed mythological reflection on the sonic essence of bodies. It allows us to conceive of an ecology, which is to say a way of inhabiting sounds, directly within language itself. Quignard's thought, under the guise of denouncing the aggression of the noises of industrial modernity, leads us to reflect on the very origin of sounds and of hearing. What does it mean to hear? What does it mean to breathe? to speak? to sing? In his writing Quignard goes to the heart of questions related to sound, the production of sounds, and our listening to them. The first theoretical condition for thinking about a sonic ecology is to admit the immanent presence of sound in every living

3. Pascal Quignard, *The Hatred of Music* (trans. Matthew Amos and Fredrik Rönnbäck; Yale University Press, 2016), 73. Translation modified.

being and to start from such a prehistory, even if it remains inaccessible to knowledge. Quignard indeed supposes a constitutive sonic foundation that has been repressed or transformed and that we no longer hear as such, for we have domesticated its power. It remains, but without expression, like a primal state, the vestige of a naked and silent childhood, utterly defenseless amid the din that has invaded it. Bodies, prior even to their humanization or personalization, have been traversed, stamped in the midst of these depths.

The sonic depths of the world

Quignard's audacious hypothesis consists in hearing recognizable sounds — syllables and notes — as covering over such a sonic substrate: They echo, formalize, and articulate these primordial sounds, these beats and vibrations, in order to make then audible and bearable. The prehistory of sound, of sound that has become listenable, goes back to the archaic flow of waves, what we might call a *geno-sound*, that precedes and remains latent in the resonances of *pheno-sounds*, which themselves are identifiable. The image Quignard gives is that of a fetus's hearing, which is subjected to the voice and the rhythms of the body that carries it:

> Intrauterine hearing is described by naturalists as remote since the placenta distances the noise of the heart and the intestines, the water reduces the intensity of the sounds, making them deeper, transporting them in large waves massaging the body. Deep in the uterus thus reigns a low and constant background noise, which acousticians compare to a "muffled whisper." The noise of the outside world itself is perceived as a "muffled, soft, low drone"

> above which rises the *melos* of the mother's voice, repeating the tonic accent, the prosody, the phrasing that she adds to the language she speaks.[4]

The sonic milieu of these depths is traversed by heterogeneous noises; it is polyrhythmic and polysensory. The maternal voice perceived by the fetus is not overvalued in this description, but is mixed with both the trivial sounds of the organic body and the buzzing of the outside world. Rather than presenting this milieu as a homogeneous and protected room, Quignard suggests that passive listening alternates between feelings of apathy and terror: Sound takes hold of the whole being; it mobilizes it and subdues it; it makes it vibrate and shakes it; it imposes a rhythm on it. From this first and inexpressive experience, there remain cries and groans that haunt the body, like those atoms of sound described by Lucretius. They continue to circulate in domesticated sounds. Listening to music or to verbal language includes this archaic savagery of indefinite and indomitable sound, a muddle always ready to invade the body, to pierce its covering and introduce the anarchy of their vibrations. According to Quignard, we speak and we sing to try to regain control over these invasive waves. Music protects us from sounds — this is his astonishing suggestion. What resounds, sings, or speaks thus comes to cover over this fundamental sound, and attentive ears know how to sense, even in the smallest hum, panic violence.

Thus defined, music and verbal language can be listened to differently. The hypothesis of an archaic sonic milieu radically changes the definition and interpretation of writing, whether musical, literary, or philosophical. It implies the listener's or reader's abandonment of meaning, or, at

4. *Ibid.*, 139.

least, it leads us to think differently about the meaning of words and sentences. Our fixation on systems of signs and structures of meaning closes our ears to these sonic depths, which nevertheless remain in our body's memory and in our memories of learning sounds. Objectivized through networks of meaning and embedded in settings that regulate anything sensory, affective, or intellectual, this sonic substratum no longer resounds, though it still resonates, perhaps, in a voice that gets altered or a rhythm that gets carried away. Quignard hears it as "semantic deposits without meaning": A residual sense was deposited into sentences and has been covered over by regulated meanings.

What would we gain by listening to this vibratory base in human languages? Doubtless we would gain access to a proto-meaning, underlying music and speech, contained in "this group of asemic sounds that disturb rational thought inside the skull and that awaken in the process a nonlinguistic memory."[5] These sonic depths are audible so long as we allow ourselves to listen to them and measure their power in our speech and thought. This pre-linguistics (or this *infra*-linguistics, for it remains under our words) determines the language that, forgetting this sonic origin, channels it through semantics, all the while secretly inheriting its rhythms. Rousseau's reflections on the beginnings of language in his *Essay on the Origin of Languages* anticipated this idea, but these sonic depths no longer belong only to those first, unarticulated voices that philosophers attribute to human passions. In a more oceanic manner, these depths concern all sounds whose beats the literary decipherer listens to. They no longer allow us to privilege only the human voice but make us put all sonic sources on equal footing and into an acoustic community with non-human animals. The vibration of the world touches and invades

5. *Ibid.*, 106.

all beings and informs all their murmurings. Vococentrism has given prevalence to human speech, heard as the first path to access meaning, to the intelligible, and to a language that could order things. But if we hear the sonic milieu behind music or words, other vibratory movements appear. We must take a step back from the anthropocentrism of discourses about the human voice to gain access to the sonic underpinnings of the world, whether they be animal, vegetal, or mineral. From there, we can recompose sonic families, without reference to species classifications. The human voice would no longer be defined by its difference from animal cries or the inept chirping of birds, as the tradition of metaphysics has always needed to do in order to mark these sounds as different and relegate them to meaninglessness. In the cacophony of sound that makes the world vibrate, all sounds, intentional or not, are supported by breaths and rhythms.

From this non-humanist conception of a fundamental sonic milieu, we can listen to what humans do with ears that are finally open. Such listening requires putting the verbal and meaning aside. Remaining fixated on the "content" of a verbal or musical phrase, seeking in it an idea, a feeling, or a message, prevents us from hearing its sonic depths. Certainly, meanings get associated, according to conventions, with this or that verbal or musical form: We can read one of Racine's alexandrines and observe its balance between love and power; we can listen to a nocturne by Chopin and experience melancholy. This direct access to the verbal or musical object, however, does not exempt readers and listeners from hearing, beyond meaning, a multitude of sonic relations that escape codes of signification. Constitutive layers at the heart of syllables and notes rustle with breaths and rhythms that precede linguistic articulation. Some writers, aware of this sonic memory, fully assume in their creations the anarchic strangeness of these noises that knock into language and thought. This is the case for Valère Novarina, who, as a playwright, has doubtless been more inclined than most other writers to hear language, allowing him to declare: "I write with my ears."[6]

Phonetic animals

To write, to think, to read with our ears ... what do such proposals mean? To be sure, they engage us in a new relation to language and to sounds. They suppose an unlearning, a disengaging from meaning in order to open our ears to sonic flow and its multiple senses. They imply an uncoupling of words from their reference, less to empty them of all content and to treat them as sonic signifiers than to allow unheard-of layers of associations with sensations, affects, imaginaries, and mental representations to emerge. To unhear, to unspeak — these are gestures that Novarina thus claims and that he asks his actors to accomplish. Rather than respecting diction, the parsing of sentences by syntax, or breathing intended to highlight the wit of meaning, Novarina demands that the breath of speech that lies beneath the syllables be brought out. Close to Artaud, but substituting existential anguish with a jubilant euphoria of language, he seeks a wild and archaic spoken language not reducible to signifying, communicating, or expressing. Treating words as sonic material that passes through bodies like the wind, he rediscovers their buried sonorities, sometimes proceeding, like Rabelais, by enumerating dialectal terms that sound at once strange and familiar to the ears of readers and listeners. A pre-linguistic sound, animalistic and dramatic, is made to resonate in words through this memory:

6. Valère Novarina, "Lettre aux acteurs" (in *Le théâtre des paroles*; P.O.L., 2007), 9: "J'écris par les oreilles."

> Heard for the first time the day before yesterday, or remembered from the depths of early childhood, strangely familiar or luminously incomprehensible, they are like animal tracks within us; [...] they play at waiting and returning, remain hidden while remembering, anticipate, rhyme or unrhyme, resound and become unsound: They remember in advance in order to think. Each word, each phonetic animal traced within us, if we wish to bring it to our ear to hear — and to listen to what it remembers — awakens the entire philological drama.[7]

The smallest word thus contains a sonic power that informs language and thought, and its echoes are perceived by speaking and listening beings more or less consciously. The suggestion of such a non-human force at work in humanity's words allows us to hear this anarchic breath that modifies the spaces and settings at the foundation of all systems of representation — signs, images, or concepts. Thinking is thus fundamentally not conceiving ideas, but first of all modifying sonic spaces and their relations. Lucretius described atoms of sound as molecular assortments that traversed bodies and gave form to verbal entities. These undulatory elements gather into words and upset acoustic equilibria. They are at the foundation of thought insofar as thought is forged in the remodeling of language, itself composed of breaths, respirations, and vibrations. Contrary to the idealist illusion that leads one to believe that thought prexists language, which would then express it, the acoustic conception of how words and ideas are formed presupposes an elementary stock of sounds from which intelligible words are constituted.

7. Valère Novarina, *La Quatrième Personne du singulier* (P.O.L., 2012), 23.

Consequently, a sonic ecology of texts and the thought they expose is based on sonic, respiratory dynamics. It listens to the contradictory flows that modify acoustic spaces and our ways of hearing words, their meaning, and the sonic replies from which they originate. That celebrated breath that must, as we showed above, be heard materially, beyond any metaphor of inspiration, is not just the one that passes through the human voice. Rather, it is, more generally, the interweaving of melodies from the sonic milieus in which we think. Thinking thus proceeds from the displacement of air masses — deflagration, gust, whisper, murmur — which transforms the auditory milieu in which words whisper to each other. Novarina, who conceives of thought in the manner of a theater where the drama of language is replayed, thus recommends:

> No ideas on stage, ever! And no ideas in thought either — but *rhythmic characters*, *instabilities*, beasts in combat — no *substances*, nor nouns, nor adjectives, nor *beings that hold together*! But *the action of the verb*, the fire of breath, burning, *consuming* every letter ... no arrangement of arranged ideas: Those are only mannequins in the store window, puppets at rest! True thoughts come in spirals, in torrents, and in whirlwinds — like so many *musical battles*.[8]

Against an idealist tradition, some philosophers have countered the definition of philosophy as the exposition or creation of ideas, concepts, notions, entities, etc., in this way, preferring verbs to nouns and qualifiers. When doing philosophy, Wittgenstein, like many others, did not seek to construct pet words with which to imprint his thoughts and bequeath them to posterity. For such philosophers, philosophy is first and foremost an activity. We could use different

8. *Ibid.*, 83–84.

terms and images to describe its movements and energies: rhythms, paths, chaos, fugues, whirlwinds, etc. Instead of conceptual "puppets" put into motion by a regulated dramaturgy of philosophy, sonic ecology allows us to hear the acoustics of thought, its displacement of air and space.

Pricking up our ears when speaking or reading is thus a new agenda, at once intellectual and sensory, to access this sonic substrate. It requires the immersion of the thinker, the actor, or the reader in the acoustic milieu of texts and thought. Speech will find other reasons and reasonings there than those concepts and syntheses that have reduced the multiplicity of meanings to a single meaning. We must reintroduce hearing (*entendre*) into understanding (*entendement*). The sonic ecology of texts is based on the fact that every speaker, and therefore every thinker, displaces sounds in a milieu that is already, for as long as can be remembered, inhabited by other speakers and other thinkers. Each emission and each reception partakes in the same acoustic substrate where masses of vibratory energies meet, come into contact, and clash with each other. Let us then listen, within texts themselves, to what this sonic ecology means. Reading with our ears implies an attention not only to sonic references, but also to the paradigmatic dimension of sound when it guides writing, whether in its movement or its ideal. Even if such listening presupposes distancing oneself from the meaning of words, it does not dismiss meaning. On the contrary, it rediscovers meaning according to a new acoustics that reveals unsuspected riches, which we will be able to hear thanks to a "third ear."

Reading "with our ears" is something we can do in multiple ways, for sound comes about in many different states. In its acoustic dimension, sound is perceptible with one or two ears. Sound is also accessible through a virtual listening when we hear sounds in our mind, which is to say that we have more or less active "ears" that mobilize virtual, but nonetheless "heard" sounds without their being hummed, according to our pleasure or the sonic traces we find in texts. And then there is what some thinkers have called a *third ear* that hears in the sense of understanding by discovering psychological and intelligible dimensions to acoustic meaning. It is this third ear that we shall describe in this last chapter.

Let's first recall sound's different natures as we can observe them in texts:

• The **voice** supposed to be at work in writing can be heard in diverse ways according to the amount of fiction the reader brings into play. This voice must not be confused with style, even if, metaphorically, it is often employed to define the writer's way of writing. "We recognize a great writer by their voice," some critics would say. Still, one author can have many voices, even when adopting only a single style. Some voices are intentional; others, not consciously adopted, speak through the writer. These are voices that are spectral, dead, or pastiched; they are voices of the writer's ethnic and social tribes or of their childhood. They are contextual voices, affected by the sonic milieus the author has traversed. To the author's voices are mixed those of the reader, whose voice too is complex, for it recruits fictions and projections onto the supposed voice of the author and their sonic identities.

• **Pseudo-acoustic phenomena** arise from writing on account of how it arranges its rhythms, intonations, and inflexions, which impose certain bodily positions on the reader. These effects principally have to do with breath. Whatever the particularities of how we read, we do not physically read Marcel Proust and Louis-Ferdinand Céline in the same way, nor Descartes and Spinoza, Marguerite Duras and Elfriede Jelinek, Henry James and James Baldwin, etc. The reader's body arranges itself differently according to the breath and rhythmics of each piece of writing. The pneumatic breath and the mental breath mingle and produce surges or syncopations or stifflings or spacings — any sensation that sets up a relation of equilibrium or disequilibrium between the body and the text. We must again make clear that readers are more or less disposed to hearing these pseudo-acoustic phenomena according to the auditory training they've received, which allows them to feel them, or even identify them.

• **Sonic referents** in a text, which is to say when a text indicates a sound, some particular noises, or a piece of music, are audible under certain conditions. The "representation" of sound remains complex, for it is generally indexed according to a visual paradigm. A reference to color or to an object stirs the imagination, and, from a single word, a mental image can seize the reader and play the role of a pseudo-perception. Sound, however, has less to do with space than with time and vibration. When it gets noticed in a text, how does it come to consciousness, and through what virtual phenomena? The expression *sonic image*, created by analogy, remains rather insufficient, for it assigns the sonic its role through the visual, depriving it of autonomy. Transcribing birdsong does not involve a bird's image. The same could be said of the wind, and this is no less true for a piece of music. Sounds make themselves heard virtually or fictionally. Reference to a lion's roar, for example, can create a fictional listening linked to the reader's memory of the lion noises they've heard, whether at the circus or at the start of a Metro-Goldwyn-Mayer film. The word used for the lion's roar itself may influence the production of such a sonic fiction, as with the onomatopoetic rumbling *r*'s of *rugissement* or *roar*.

• The **signifiers of a language** too resound within so-called silent reading. Their sounds depend on both phonetic codes and the ears of readers who listen to them in different ways. On the one hand, the phonemes that constitute signifiers form minimal units that determine the sound of a language. On the other hand, their pronunciation, and therefore the way they are heard, depends on the speech and culture of the reader. The sonic dimension of words, as poetry makes manifest, is at once obvious and complex, notably when it concerns the relations between a natural sound and the sound meant to imitate it. Racine's famous verse *Pour qui sont ces serpents qui sifflent sur vos têtes* ? — "For whom are these snakes that hiss atop your heads?" — is supposed to make the sound of a snake heard through these alliterating *s*'s that imitate it. And yet, what we hear is the sound of a snake as the word imposes it, as if, in reality, the animal were imitating the sound that our language has attributed to it. The variety of words from language to language that specify noises underlines the complex associations between words and sounds. Signifiers, in their sonic dimension, induce soundscapes that are related more to their language than to the referent represented.

• **Metaphors** carry meanings through sonic references. We can see this with barking: "He barked at me" refers to the symbolism we attribute to dogs and to the sounds they emit. The use of such analogies reveals a transfer of meaning through a musical and sonic lexicon. It oscillates between symbolic and metaphorical, depending on whether a sound gets erected as the univocal representative of some reality or whether it invents one association among heterogeneous realities. Still, a metaphor is always complex and must be deciphered, for it contains values, ideologies, and affects at many levels. The use of the verb *to bark* thereby implies the depreciation of the animal that barks, enclosing it in the sonic sphere of noise and animality (*bêtise*, 'stupidity', literally 'beastliness'). More positively, musical metaphors are most often founded on an idea of harmony and function according to assumptions stemming as much from the subjective pleasure of listening as from commonplaces about music.

• **Soundscapes**, in a text, are more or less random compositions of natural or artificial sounds forming a coherent ensemble. The *-scape* of *soundscape* (*paysage sonore*) comes from *landscape* (*paysage*) and is doubtless overly tied to a visual paradigm, all the more so since sound overwhelmingly proceeds through the immersion of a passive listener, unlike vision, which is objective and spectator-centric. And so we might prefer other terms, like sonic *milieu*. The description of soundscapes or sonic milieus in a text puts into relief sounds, noises, and musics as such. Still, such descriptions risk fetishizing sound if it is not linked to other sensations or surrounding elements. Sound is indeed never alone, but always in relation to spaces of listening and auditory cultures. This is not just about pseudo-synesthetic sensations that mix hearing with sight, smell, touch, or even taste, but also about imagination and intellection. A soundscape contains complex, non-intentional meanings, connections, and connotations: This is how the play of affinities operates to link heterogeneous elements that, in combination, create a soundscape. Sounds, through their dynamics, are woven together with a multitude of images, thoughts, affective situations, and sensory phenomena — all those interlacings that literature can describe so well.

The sense of sound

The question we have been trying to answer since we started listening in on theoretical texts can be summarized as follows: Do the sounds we hear when reading texts have meaning? This inquiry can be extended: Do they have a meaning of their own, or do they participate in a network of meanings? Do they reveal meanings that only hearing can discover? Or are they but secondary, even pernicious, effects of language? Voices have been thus accused of diverting the listener from the message intended for them. The distrust of sonic meaning comes from those who adhere to there being a meaning proper to a sound. These are mainly philosophers who oppose, on the one hand, reason, *logos*, and content, and, on the other, voice, style, and ornament. The willful deafness of these abstract thinkers, as we saw at the outset of our investigation, is meant to allow exclusive concentration on the message, idea, or essence. Such a desire to repress sound, however, arouses our curiosity, and then our suspicion: Why mustn't we hear? What shouldn't we hear? Why is the Sirens' song deadly? In the face of such fear and the antitheses it generates to contain it, a different listening is possible … and desirable, a listening that would not separate meaning from its vocal utterance and its multiple sonic dimensions. It suffices to observe that a dissonant intonation, a vocal accident can work against the explicit meaning of a word and reveal something rather different from its initial meaning. Just as bodily gestures can expose lies, a stammer, an obsessive repetition, an excessively loud volume, an unusual intensity, or a strange pitch can sometimes make audible the opposite of the discourse being put forward. It is therefore important to think of meaning and sound together and to confer on sound a function other than that of "expression," accompaniment, or instrumentation (as when we use expressions like "vocal instrument," or even "vocal organ," thereby reducing voice to the larynx and the vocal cords).

Do sounds in a musical or verbal composition possess autonomous meaning? We must distinguish here between two meanings: the meaning that we attribute to sounds (for example, the sadness of a violin chord or of raindrops) and the meaning that would come from the sounds themselves, if we accept the hypothesis of immanent meaning. When it comes to music, the answer might be yes, they can: Composed sounds seem to us to have a meaning at once transcendent and immanent. A requiem, as a liturgical form, remains bound to the theme of death and, even in those parts devoid of sung words, bears the mark of a prayer for the deceased. The same requiem, however, can be listened to as a piece of music, independent of its "theme," either by appreciating its composition and formal structure, or by associating it with feelings other than those intended by the composer. To this point, Clément Rosset, denouncing the idea of an expressive meaning to music, demonstrates that a work can be heard and interpreted in contrary ways if we reverse the meaning of its words without changing its music: Thus, in the famous aria sung by Orpheus in Gluck's opera *Orphée et Eurydice*, if we replace "J'ai perdu mon Eurydice" ("I have lost my Eurydice") with

"J'ai trouvé mon Eurydice" ("I have found my Eurydice"), the flow and immanent "meaning" of the music would not be altered,[1] and the associated feelings could change from nostalgia to joy.

Our goal is to hear sounds in texts, and we will not enter the debates between those who uphold music's meaning (where music would convey feelings and ideas), those who defend its non-expressivity (where music would not express anything by itself), or those who consider music to be like a language (where music would be open to semiology). Nevertheless, the hypothesis that some meaning could come from sounds themselves concerns us here in the extreme in order to access some secondary meaning beyond the semantics of a text. We can observe, at the least, that all meanings we habitually attribute to sounds are "imported." These sounds — melancholic, joyful, spiritual, etc. — are affected by meaning, whence the impression that they naturally express feelings like pain, terror, joy, etc. Nevertheless, any such association between sounds and sentiments remains the result of convention. The settings of convention induce, in effect, a group of listeners to feel the same emotions when listening to certain sonic compositions, while people from other cultures would not. Wittgenstein thus remarked that a human being who has not received the same auditory training as some group for whom certain musical works are familiar may hear sonic coherence, but will not feel it with the same affects and meaning, and, above all, this individual will not have the language to talk about it:

1. Clément Rosset, *L'invisible* (Minuit, 2012), 27.

> Might one not imagine someone who had never known music, and who came to us and heard someone playing a reflective piece of Chopin, being convinced that this was a language and people were merely keeping the sense secret from him?[2]

In some way, this music seems to him to "speak," but as a listener he would lack the link between sounds, themes, and meanings. For meaning is conventional insofar as it is a web of relations at the heart of a culture, and sounds have no natural vocation, even when composed, to express universal meanings or feelings.

As for words and their sounds, what about meanings that could come from sound itself? It is not as easy to separate sound and meaning in language as it is in music, for words are not notes, and they refer, by their referential nature, to realities filled with affects and images. Nevertheless, as Wittgenstein again remarked: "What we call 'understanding a sentence' has, in many cases, a much greater similarity to understanding a musical theme than we might be inclined to think."[3] Yet again we should distinguish *understanding* and *hearing*, for they do not have exactly the same meaning when it comes to verbal language and to music. While music operates without signs, language exists as a system of signs. Understanding languages in its utterances and enunciations implies taking account of the relations that have been instituted between sounds, signifieds, and signifiers. Without reducing sounds to signs, we must confront the complex relations that sound maintains to the meanings of words. The sounds of a language or of a particular piece of writing indeed produce a sort of sonic

2. Ludwig Wittgenstein, *Remarks on the Philosophy of Psychology* (trans. G. E. M. Anscombe; University of Chicago Press, 1980), §I-888.
3. Ludwig Wittgenstein, *The Blue and Brown Books* (Harper Torchbooks, 1965), 167.

and semantic layering at the heart of sentences we "understand," and there they arrange multiple networks of meanings and expressions. It is here that reading with our ears, and not just our eyes or our deaf intellect, gives us access to semantic layers in a text other than its explicit meaning. Through these language games, we apprehend, with a great deal of indetermination, some object or idea through the selection, superposition, or condensation of meanings. This is one of the reasons why Wittgenstein, as a philosopher, embraced the use of "vague concepts" when confronted with the definitional illusion of ontological concepts. To be sure, understanding a word or a sentence implies vagueness, opacity, and movement. If we hear *other*, *greenery*, *liberty*, *ethics*, etc., it is less that we employ some operation of synthesis on the word's manifest diversity than that we operate a logical selection from among its possible extensions of meaning: It sounds the same or resonates in the same way, but nothing is certain. We proceed via affinities of meanings, and the relations between the realities designated by these vagues concepts owe more to "family resemblances" — as familial airs, musical scores playing on known associations — than to any veritable identify of meaning.

The third ear

If understanding can resemble listening to a musical melody, then the meaning of texts calls out for a new sense of hearing, what thinkers sensitive to sounds have sometimes named a "third ear." Nietzsche boasted of having one, which allowed him to hear more precisely and more profoundly the meaning of philosophical texts, for better or worse.[4] To hear more and better than others gives one

4. Friedrich Nietzsche, *Beyond Good and Evil* (trans. Walter Kaufmann; Vintage, 1966), §246.

access to the musicality of the world and its languages, but also reveals the heaviness of words and thoughts that do not sing — the sign of simple minds. Settling scores, Nietzsche observed that the style of German philosophy was indifferent to timbre, written for the eyes and not the ears. Readers of such barely sonic writing, lacking an auditory culture, forget that they have a sense of hearing, whereas the Ancients read aloud, for texts seemed to them full of sound and understandable through declamation. For Nietzsche, they possessed a culture of the ear, larynx, and lungs.

Freud took up this idea of a third ear to characterize how the analyst listens. Auditory attention is indeed not the monopoly of music-loving thinkers, like Nietzsche, who know how to perceive the auditory meaning of sentences. It also comes from a method applicable to psychoanalysis, which can export its radically innovative conception of reading to other domains. Freud did not theorize it at length, but it is at the foundation of analytic practice. What does it mean to hear, to listen to, and to understand a patient, or rather an analysand, who works on meaning as a process, bringing forth unintentional meanings that come from the unconscious? Freud's practical reflections are of interest to us here in at least two ways: They allow us to hear a meaning other than explicit meaning; and they call into question any listening to or reception of this meaning.

The first transgression that Freud suggests regarding meaning has to do with its understanding and interpretation. In fact, he challenges our desire to understand, though this would seem to go without saying for an analyst is supposed uncover the causes of suffering along the model of a reader who must decipher a text. It is precisely this model of understanding that is not pertinent to the analyst (and Wittgenstein would challenge it for sentences as well).

Freud observed that, in the early days of psychoanalysis, he had remained prisoner to an intellectualist conception of mental illness, giving knowledge too much credit: He put himself to finding information on the patient, gathering it from various sources, and seeking to identify some repressed childhood trauma.[5] The protocol for understanding thus rested on the idea of knowledge that could potentially be shared between analyst and patient. His objective was to establish a diagnosis communicable to the analysand. Nevertheless, their resistances always kept them from attaining the entirety of the knowledge needed. Freud thus discovered that the meaning of this knowledge had to be kept to the side, despite the analyst's intense desire to understand, in order to allow the phenomena of transference to operate, lifting the analysand's resistances and letting other truths emerge. He became aware of this, all the more so as he too involved his own unconscious in his relation to his patients and to the formulation of these truths.

The governing word for this new attitude toward meaning that Freud recommended was "suspension." One must indeed suspend the will to understanding, to find a meaning, to pounce on important information, and to select the essential while leaving aside the superfluous. All of these operations predispose us to knowledge and make us miss elements that would later be revealed as determinative. It is thus important to leave all words and all information in equal suspension, even if they seem secondary on a first listening. Freud thereby defined the attitude of the analyst, who must adopt "free-floating attention" (*gleichschwebende Aufmerksamkeit*, 'evenly-suspended attention'; in French as *attention flottante*). Instead of following his own

5. See Sigmund Freud, "On Beginning the Treatment" (*The Standard Edition* vol. 12, trans. James Strachey; The Hogarth Press, 1958), 141.

inclinations, which were as much the product of his learned intellect as they were of his unconscious tendencies, Freud received what he heard and let it float about. He suspended his knowledge and his intent to understand: He listened to the patient with his third ear.

To listen before understanding (or believing one understands), before explaining and interpreting, is to avoid being duped by one's own intelligence, which is but the confirmation of a meaning forged in advance of the analysis. For this reason, Freud asks analysts to take as few notes as possible during sessions and to preserve their free-floating listening. They will then become receivers of the patient's unconscious, without imposing either their judgments or their objections. Freud then uses the *telephone model* to describe this type of attention:

> He must turn his own unconscious like a receptive organ toward the transmitting unconscious of the patient. He must adjust himself to the patient as a telephone receiver is adjusted to the transmitting microphone. Just as the receiver converts back into sound waves the electric oscillations in the telephone line which were set up by sound waves, so the doctor's unconscious is able, from the derivatives of the unconscious which are communicated to him, to reconstruct that unconscious, which has determined the patient's free associations.[6]

The third ear is thus like a telephone receiver, and the passivity of its reception allows it to hear and connect the sound waves it receives. It defines the conduct of the analyst and, more generally, of any listening that is receptive to aleatory meanings, which would then not get excluded or reduced by one's unhearing intellect.

6. *Ibid.*, 115–16.

Following Freud, the psychoanalyst Theodor Reik highlighted how much this third ear allowed one to hear people's voices, breaths, rhythms, and music. In his 1949 *Listening with the Third Ear: The Inner Experience of a Psychoanalyst*, Reik affirmed that, in a psychoanalytic session, the sound of the saying is more important that what is said. The content of meaning focuses our attention, but with a free-floating listening, we can reach the music of speech and its dynamic, relational meanings. The composer Gustav Mahler said that what was most important was not in the score. The psychoanalyst too must open their ears to what gets missed in meanings and to what escapes signs. Stifling the desire to understand, the analyst sets themselves to listening to the tiniest phenomena, the smallest breath, and lapses in rhythm. As Reik wrote:

> The analyst, like his patient, knows things without knowing that he knows them. The voice that speaks in him, speaks low, but he who listens with a third ear hears also what is expressed almost noiselessly, what is said *pianissimo*.[7]

Soundwaves enter discretely through one ear, leave the other, and come back in through the third, carrying a fugitive material that only an acute hearing can capture. This third ear hears what is not said aloud, but gets diffused through microsounds. It hears as well those spectral voices that speak in counterpoint and are habitually inaudible because they are covered over by the speech of conscious thought. Can such listening be applied to reading texts? Does free-floating attention also give access to meanings that come through hearing? Freud himself practiced this type of reading beyond the setting of the analytic session.

7. Theodor Reik, *Listening with the Third Ear: The Inner Experience of a Psychoanalyst* (Farrar, Straus and Company, 1949), 145.

The suspension of meaning seems contrary to an intelligent reading of argumentative texts. And yet, it is a condition for accessing meanings that are at times contradictory to what is explicitly proposed. This attitude certainly goes against our reading habits, which privilege comprehension, by putting aside our anxieties about not grasping an argument immediately: When we don't understand something we feel rejected as stupid, as outside acceptable norms or logic; we think we are like Alcibiades who hears in Socrates's discourse only the sound of a flute.[8] We hold fast to understanding, for we recognize ourselves in comprehension, which confirms our participation in reason and in the language that orders the word. Abstract texts demand this controlled reading all the more since they arise from a will to master meaning and from a belief in the absolute power of naming ("I call this X," "I maintain that ...," "Y is ...") and literal meaning. When Freud read philosophical texts, he adopted suspension in order to hear something other than conceptual and argumentative assertion. Although he was very interested in philosophy — he wrote texts that today we consider philosophical — he nevertheless read philosophy at a certain remove, distrustful of its general truths, suspecting they had psychological motivations.

What then might it mean to read philosophy with a third ear? For the analyst, it means hearing the affective causes of abstract discourse, and more particularly in such discourses that present worldviews. The will to give a general meaning imagines a unicity of all things, and, above all, it presupposes that one meaning reigns over them.

8. Embracing such a listening to the musicality of thought, Foucault used to say that he heard Lacan's speech as music. Philippe Roger, recalling Roland Barthes's seminars, but having forgotten the words of a particular utterance, wrote: "I could transcribe its rhythm in quarter notes, eighth notes, rests, and bar lines." Philippe Roger, *Roland Barthes, roman* (Grasset, 1986), 3.

Philosophers, Freud observed, cannot accept that a thing or situation, a status or action has no meaning.[9] Their conceptual production therefore comes from several psychic drives: a fear of emptiness, which leads them to want to fill in gaps of meaning; a narcissistic overestimation of their intellectual interventions, which leads them to believe in the omnipotence of thought; a magical belief in the power of words to institute meaning, which likens their speech to that of the religious. This analysis is severe and concerns only a certain type of philosophical discourse; however, it suggests to us that we not hear the weighty words, concepts, and reasons of abstract discourse per se but listen to the complex work of sublimation found therein. It locates the pleasure at work in the enunciation of ideas and tracks its pet words, what Adorno called *Stichwort*: reality at once eliminated and ennobled by concepts.[10] It is not necessary to take up the Freudian theory of the unconscious to perceive these psychic investments in language. There is no need to presuppose a "text's unconscious" and claim to decypher its logic, which would risk reducing sound yet again to a simple expressive function. Listening to texts discovers instead pluridimensional psychic movements that arise from grafting words and sounds and that diffuse contradictory forces in putting forth and writing down concepts that are imposing, trenchant, menacing, etc.

To hear this imperious and/or deadly voice, one must sometimes deform the sound of words, such that they lose their captivating power and come to resound oddly, revealing their correlations with other words subject to the same driving force. The repetition of certain phrases, a rise in

9. See Sigmund Freud, "The Question of a *Weltanschauung*" (*The Standard Edition* vol. 22, trans. James Strachey; The Hogarth Press, 1964).
10. See Theodor Adorno, *The Jargon of Authenticity* (trans. Knut Tarnowski and Frederic Will; Northwestern University Press, 1973).

tone, an intense articulation ... the listener or reader perceives these small phenomena by taking a step back. Discourse is thus tapped,[11] such that it reveals something other than its explicit meaning: the stigmas of thought. Nathalie Sarraute, who was the great master of underconversations (*sous-conversations*), had that fine sense of hearing able to reveal tropisms, whether unavowed desire or deadly violence, at the heart of the most anodyne sentences. Her play *Isma* makes us hear how certain words bear sonic drives and produce devastating effects on those who listen to them. In the following conversation, Sarraute points out a compulsive use of the suffix *-ism* (emphasized in speech as *-isma*, in French, and *-isem*, in English), which alone can transform an ordinary word into a doctrine:

> HIM: *Isem* ... when you follow it to its source ... it leads us ...
> HER, *quietly*: To the unspeakable. Which has no name. Which is nowhere expected. Which nothing prohibits.
> HIM: Something slippery ... which slips through your fingers.
> HER: We catch it for an instant. Romantic*ism*. Capital*ism*. Syndical*ism*. Structural*ism*. It's that ending in *-isem*. It straightens it up. It's like a scorpions tail. It stings us ... it discharges its venom into us ... to punish us ... just for these words ... for their suffixes.[12]

11. This is the word (in French as *mettre sur écoute*) that David Christoffel used when he "tapped" Foucault's voice and used software to find, across hundreds of hours of audio recordings, phenomena of melody, rhythm, or timbre, which made the schemas that drove his thought audible. From these, Christoffel made an "acousmatic work" presented at IRCAM in 2014.
12. Nathalie Sarraute, *Isma ou ce qui s'appelle rien* (in Œuvres complètes; Bibliothèque de la Pléiade, 1996), 1445.

Enunciating or accentuating a syllable brings about vibrations that change the meaning of words and inscribe them into the tropism of intersubjective relations. The sonic charge of suffixes like *-ism*, *-ty*, or *-tion* (*-isme*, *-té*, or *-tion* in French) pronounces the violence of the concept. It is thus of the utmost use to a reader to hear, depending on the text, how a thinker's pet words emerge and get repeated and asserted. Concepts indeed carry a punch. They mark sentences with their sonic imprint, and the way they are struck says a lot about their author's thinking. Listening to philosophical texts with a third ear will hear the drama of ideas and arguments: Certain concepts make their appearance to fanfare, while others arise *mezza voce*; some cry out, as Deleuze observed, while others whisper. This acoustic reception of texts with a third ear makes the case for a "second listening" to philosophy.[13] It consists in a provisional stay of verbal meaning to give passive attention to sonic phenomena and to things within earshot that transport affects. It can then hear secondary truths, sometimes in contradiction to the explicit message; it can discover that the text might be the symptom of a lived experience contrary to what is being emphasized philosophically. Underlayers of meaning are perceived beyond the master's voice and its assertive drive, its *libido affirmandi*.

The reader's tertiary voice

The meanings that emerge when listening to a text, whether heard or read, nevertheless depend on our ability to mobilize our third ear. The sounds of a text produce meanings subjacent to its explicit discourse, but they are not audible in the same way for every reader. Indeed, while the ability to hear is widely shared, it entails distinct cultures and

13. I sought to formulate the principles of this "second listening" in *Le génie du mensonge* (Pocket, 2017).

ways of listening. It is not a matter of different degrees of hearing, but of the ear's training that leads any listener, even the "hard of hearing," to perceive sounds differently, *to listen* to them *as*. We are always liable to be in the situation of Wittgenstein's imagined Huron who, upon hearing music whose harmonic foundation is utterly unknown to him, says to himself, without feeling anything or making any associations, "It's saying something."

A second listening thus suggests a phono-acoustic relation between the reader and the text's author in which the auditory culture of one becomes accommodated, more or less, to that of the other. The same listener or reader can also adopt distinct modes of listening. During a radio program in 1979 devoted to Schumann, Claude Maupomé asked Roland Barthes: "How do you hear it?" Instead of some musicological commentary that we might have expected from Barthes, who had already written at length about Schumann's music, for Schumann was his favorite composer, he replied: "I hear it as I love it, and perhaps you will ask me 'How do you love it?', well, that I cannot answer, because I will say that I love it precisely with that part of myself that is unknown to me." The fact that Barthes, the great expert of semiology, refused to perform an analysis of signs, that he moreover disputed the idea that music was a language and expressed his personal taste for "insignificant" music — these surprising statements lead us to concede that there are several types of listening, each as legitimate as any other. *Hearing it as*: This is the disposition of the listener who doesn't so much attain some sonic object as adopt, according to circumstances, an attitude favoring now knowledge, now affect, and then again, at other times, a back-and-forth between the two. It is not always possible to account for a type of listening or for the effects produced by music. Hearing a text also suggests a disposition to listen that depends on the affects, sensibilities, memories, and imagination of the listener. We must therefore ask ourselves with which ears — the third or yet others still — does the reader hear the sonic phenomena of a text and their underlying layers of meaning. Though a second listening, in its first stages, is floating and passive, it is nonetheless determinative, for it implicates the at once collective and intimate culture of the listening subject, which is to say all the other ears that have heard the world of noises before their own have. From among the spectrum of voices that populate the listener's memory, several present themselves.

Indeed, every utterance entails some transfer of voices, which are activated by reading. A polyphony runs through texts, even those that seem the most univocal. Who speaks and whom do we hear in writing? Every written voice is adopted and composed, for there is no such thing as one's own voice. *Ça parle*, it speaks, and *ça entend*, it hears, through echoes and in all directions during reading, unbeknownst to the reader. Vocal multiplicities intertwine: those of the enunciator and those of the reader. What do we hear, for example, when we read an author from antiquity? What voice reaches us from the orator Cicero? His texts cannot be read without his beautiful eloquence creating the fiction of speech. And yet, if we are not specialists of Latin, we might know little about his voice and the rhythm of his way of speaking. Certain writings call for a kind of conversation with the reader, or even a form of sonic empathy. This is the case with Montaigne's *Essays*, which address the reader, make the reader their witness, and treat the reader as both a philosophical interlocutor and confidant. We hear Montaigne's voice, but which one? With which accent? And even if we know how certain words from that time were pronounced, we do not have the same sense of hearing to hear them with: Ears that have heard airplane engines or the electrified voices of the Rolling Stones cannot hear the sounds of nature or the voices of Guyenne countryfolk like those of a sixteenth-century reader could. Nevertheless we doubtless hear a voice that is Montaigne's, though fictional, of course, and based on our own, like a voice used by an actor. We fictionalize a speaking Montaigne, and we hear him speaking to us with this composite voice.

The artifices introduced by this phono-acoustic relation of the reader to the text are redoubled in translation. Indeed, when we read texts originally written in a language other than our own, similar fictions haunt our reading. Our language imposes a sampling of possible voices, which have breaths, rhythms, and soundscapes different from those of other languages. We hear these foreign texts both as we believe they sounded in certain spaces and in certain eras and as they resonate now in our own, familiar milieu. Thus, Yukio Mishima's voice, in his masterpiece tetralogy *The Sea of Fertility*, goes through two translations to reach a French reader, first from Japanese to English and then from English to French. A Japanese reader already hears composite voices in this text, not only those that Mishima puts into play in each of the four novels, but also those that employ archaisms and Chinese references. It is then heard by a French reader through a number of sieves layered between what they read and their own ears. Reading thereby induces a composite and projective listening to the characters' voices in a novel, just as it does for its soundscapes.

A transferential relation between an author and a reader is at work in the act of reading through the polyphony of fictional voices. Among these voices speak those of the unconscious, with its filters and its willful deafness.

The comparison Freud proposed between listening analyst and telephone receiver puts us on the trail of these transfers and counter-transfers: Sonic signals circulate as vibrations transcribed into voices, but also connecting two unconsciouses who listen to each other, with their reciprocal and anachronistic malentendus (the author foresees a listening that the reader believes they themselves are embodying). For there is no objectivity to these voices, despite what linguistic positivism holds, especially in a text that provokes its reader to reinvent an acoustic and sonic coherence. The reader is indeed an approximate listener who recomposes and fictionalizes, from their sonic memory, the voices they hear acousmatically. The reader therefore brings in a sort of third character who will play the role of a transferential voice. This *character-voice* is neither the author's voice nor the reader's, but a vocal arrangement that, in the little chamber play of reading, stages a scene of listening. To be sure, the character-voice can owe something to the author's acoustic voice if that voice has already been heard: If we have listened to Simone de Beauvoir in her radio broadcasts, her timbre will probably resonate when we read her memoirs or her treatise, *The Second Sex*. If we have heard Marguerite Duras giving her directors a lesson in how her texts should be read, it would be difficult for us when reading them not to adopt her rather particular rhythm, her way of making each phrase, even the most insignificant, resonate.

The character-voice is relational and inventive. Whether it incorporates an author's voice known to the reader, or whether it composes a grain and flow for a voice the reader supposes to be in harmony with the author's, this third voice is arranged in a textual score constituted by sounds, which are themselves associated with images and meaning. Thus, as we have observed, a text is never silent, but diffuses to attentive ears sounds that we "hear as," which is to say as we believe them to resonate in a particular age and in a particular space, just as they resonate now in our own, familiar milieu. Doubtless this listening comes about through misunderstanding, through malentendus; nevertheless, it establishes conditions for understanding. It sets up a relational acoustic that gives access to the sonic world of a text. When we read Cyrano de Bergerac's *The Other World: Comical History of the States and Empires of the Moon*, which was published in 1657, we might sometimes hear sounds from space movies, including synthesizer sounds, which have become imprinted on our minds as the twentieth-century sonic cliché for galactic music. Soundscapes thus get composed in reading according to our arbitrary auditory memories and their associations.

A text sings or buzzes, and we hear it as ... as we love it, or as we believe it speaks or sounds. Proust described his impression of being able to hum the sounds of a text whose musical particularity he thought he had perceived:

> When I began to read an author I very soon caught the tune of the song beneath the words, which in each author is distinct from that of every other; and while I was reading, and without knowing what I was doing, I hummed it over, hurrying the words, or slowing them down, or suspending them, in order to keep time with the rhythm of the notes, as one does in singing, where in compliance with the shape of the tune one often delays for a long time before coming to the last syllable of a word.[14]

Proust attributed this gift to his ear, which was "sharper and truer than is common." At first glance, his reflections seem to reiterate the analogy between style and music,

14. Marcel Proust, *Contre Saint-Beuve* (trans. Sylvia Townsend Warner, in *Marcel Proust on Art and Literature*; Dell Publishing, 1958), 265.

where a music-loving reader identifies and even anticipates the modes of harmonic necessity: Such a reader hears the cadence and chromaticism of sentences perfectly, making this music their own and being able to imitate it (which is what allowed Proust to write pastiches), enjoying slowing down its sonic coda. Still, two ears are at work here — refined and cultivated ears, to be sure — and they stick to the musicality of language. And yet, Proust connects this auditory gift to another, that of discovering deep links between two ideas, links that are not immediately accessible through reasoning. He observes about himself that, curiously, it is when he is most ill, even "with neither strength nor idea in my head left," that this ability works best. In this way, a meaning other than the explicit one is discovered: a revelatory association that the reader has grasped without resorting to comprehension or interpretation. Proust highlights two talents that are also two essential faculties for any reader: hearing and associating. Without using the expression, he is describing here the "third ear," which, through sounds, accesses a second meaning:

> And I think the young man who amuses himself in me like this must be the same as he whose sharp true ear can likewise distinguish a subtle harmony that others are deaf to between two impressions or two ideas.[15]

Illness and childhood insouciance are two modes of suspending the willfulness of explanatory reason. They thus allow attention to float, which, by letting sounds buried under verbal meaning come forth, then perceives the breath of meaning, its inspiration through the sonic milieu. When Proust says a little further on that books are the children

15. *Ibid.*, 266.

of silence, he suggests that the intention to speak and communicate is not the seat of meaning. On the contrary, the meaning of things happens when speech does not cover over voices and the associations they carry. Reading with our ears, through this quasi-childlike listening not yet crushed by explanation, leads us to hear these voicescapes, which give off the pensive sonority of texts.

We began this inquiry of the auditory dimension of thought by bringing the voice back to the materiality of sound, and we now find this voice immersed in soundscapes where unheard harmonies and unexpected meanings are discovered. This itinerary through the inner ears of certain writers, thinkers, and readers has led to the recognition of different types of musical, sonic, and environmental listening like so many gauges and tuning forks of textual meaning. The suggestion that hearing is not reducible to perceiving sounds, even if perceptual attention is a minimal requirement, is intended to counter the willful deafness of abstract thinkers. Listening, as we have suggested through the different paths of this investigation, entails a multiplication of ears, those that perceive, those that distract our will to understand, and those that hear second meanings. Such listening mobilizes auditory memories, which is to say ways of hearing, of attending to one noise rather than another, of prioritizing sounds, and of situating oneself in communal sonic spaces. And, above all, this essentially relational listening makes us hear that sounds are never alone and that they are connected to a number of other phenomena: images, sensations, memories, meanings, etc.

To read and to think with our ears opens up fields of investigation in any number of disciplines beyond music or acoustics. History, literature, and philosophy, in particular, would be enriched by finding the sonic dimension of their objects of study, the role music plays in them as a driving force, and the dynamics of breath and rhythm that govern ideas and languages. It is time to develop sound studies in these scholarly fields that are still too marked by the predominance of the visual or willfully deaf to and dismissive of the sonic. This listening opens out onto a multiplicity of paths, just like multi-track editing: The composite voice, the role of accents, the disruption of sounds in thought, the changes to speech due to new audio devices, soundscapes and their relational fabric — these are also realities that reveal layers to reading and understanding. We inhabit sound, we write and we think in sound, whence the necessity for a sonic ecology of societies, thoughts, and texts. Rather than merely being subjected to this immersion, we can become aware of the powers of hearing and thereby no doubt be reborn through our ears.

Dépôt légal : novembre 2025 - N° imprimeur : 112582989

Imprimé en France par Présence Graphique - Monts.